BETTER HOMES AND GAR

Step·By·Step Successful Gardening

Lawns, Ground Covers & Vines

Janet H. Sanchez

Better Homes and Gardens® Books

Des Moines

BETTER HOMES AND GARDENS® BOOKS
An Imprint of Meredith® Books

Step-By-Step Successful Gardening:
Lawns, Ground Covers & Vines
Senior Editor: Marsha Jahns
Production Manager: Douglas Johnston

Vice President and Editorial Director: Elizabeth P. Rice
Executive Editor: Kay Sanders
Art Director: Ernest Shelton
Managing Editor: Christopher Cavanaugh

President, Book Group: Joseph J. Ward
Vice President, Retail Marketing: Jamie L. Martin
Vice President, Direct Marketing: Timothy Jarrell

Meredith Corporation
Chairman of the Executive Committee: E. T. Meredith III
Chairman of the Board and Chief Executive Officer:
  Jack D. Rehm
President and Chief Operating Officer: William T. Kerr

Produced by ROUNDTABLE PRESS, INC.
Directors: Susan E. Meyer, Marsha Melnick
Executive Editor: Amy T. Jonak
Editorial Director: Anne Halpin
Senior Editor: Jane Mintzer Hoffman
Design: Sisco & Evans, New York
Photo Editor: Marisa Bulzone
Assistant Editor: Alexis Wilson
Assistant Photo Editor: Carol Sattler
Editorial Production: Don Cooper
Encyclopedia Editor: Henry W. Art and Storey Communi-
  cations, Inc., Pownal, Vermont
Horticultural Consultant: Christine M. Douglas
Copy Editor: Sue Heinemann
Proofreader: Cathy Peck
Step-by-Step Photography: Derek Fell

All of us at Meredith® Books are dedicated to providing you
with the information and ideas you need for successful
gardening. We guarantee your satisfaction with this book for
as long as you own it. If you have any questions, comments,
or suggestions, please write to us at:

MEREDITH® BOOKS, *Garden Books*
Editorial Department, RW240
1716 Locust St.
Des Moines, IA 50309-3023

If you would like to order additional copies of any of our
books, call 1-800-678-2803 or check with your local
bookstore.

Library of Congress Catalog Card Number: 94-74292
ISBN: 0-696-20212-3

Lawns, Ground Covers & Vines

Lawns, Ground Covers & Vines

Creating a garden involves many choices, whether you start with an empty plot around a new house or rework parts of an older garden. Some of the most important choices have to do with garden "floors" and "walls"—the lawns, ground covers, and vines that are the basic structural elements of the garden. • Should you have a lawn on your property? If so, how much lawn? Perhaps ground covers would be a better choice, but which ground covers? Vines can solve problems such as bare fences and unsightly views into neighbors' yards, but you may not know which vines will grow well on your property or how to plant them. • This book will answer these and other questions by discussing each type of plant in turn. You will learn to choose, plant, and care for lawns, ground covers, and vines using environmentally sensitive methods, and the result will be an enduring, unique, and beautiful garden.

To reduce maintenance, an expanse of parklike lawn surrounding the house is left uncluttered, enhanced only by a bed of annuals bounded by a low stone wall.

Traditionally lawns have occupied a large portion of most American properties. Lawns are usually such an unquestioned aspect of the American home that it is strange to think of them as an acquired taste—but they are. Our love of lawns derives from the landscape preferences brought by English settlers, who favored parklike expanses of grass as a verdant setting for their homes. Following suit, Americans have routinely surrounded their homes with lawns, even though harsher climates in the United States make the successful cultivation of grass more difficult than in the mild, moist climate of England. Until recently, a soft green expanse of grass was as essential to the civilized look of a home as a floor is to the plan of a house.

However, over the past decade or so, many Americans have begun to question the value of these extensive—and expensive—lawns. Because it is inherently unnatural, a lawn can demand a lot of time, energy, and money. You have to fertilize and irrigate the grass to make it grow, then cut it when it grows too tall—and repeat the process over and over in an endless cycle.

Maintaining a lawn can also have negative effects on the environment. For example, in many areas lawns must be irrigated frequently to survive naturally rainless summers, squandering increasingly scarce water supplies. Also, the many expensive chemicals used to maintain a lush, weed- and pest-free lawn may escape to pollute groundwater and also harm beneficial soil organisms. To add to the damage, most lawn mowers use two-cycle gasoline-powered engines, which cause noise as well as air and earth pollution. Mowing produces grass clippings, which are routinely bagged and sent to landfills. Finally, a lawn is an overly simple and artificial planting, composed almost entirely of one species; it thus lacks the biodiversity found in more natural environments. This biodiversity preserves plant communities and allows other creatures to thrive.

Homeowners across the country are experimenting with new approaches to lawns that make them less labor-intensive and less harmful to the environment. One such approach is simply to reduce the size of the lawn, retaining only as much grass as is really needed for a specific purpose, such as children's play. It's also helpful to switch to kinds of grasses that are adapted to local conditions; in recent years many drought-tolerant and disease-resistant varieties have been introduced. Another tactic is to change maintenance methods—mow and fertilize less frequently, use organic rather than chemical fertilizers, accept a few weeds in the lawn rather than reach for an herbicide, and let clippings decompose naturally. All these strategies help make lawns more environmentally acceptable.

▼ **Alternatives to Lawn**

Some gardeners have opted out of lawns altogether. There are many beautiful and practical ways to carpet your garden floors besides planting the ubiquitous lawn grass. You might try a ground cover (see page 9) or choose one of the following lawn alternatives (discussed further in Chapter One).

Meadows and prairies employ native species of ornamental grasses and wildflowers to re-create natural ecosystems.

Patios and decks are nonliving floors that are more expensive to install than a lawn but last for years with a minimum of maintenance. They provide level, open outdoor space.

Mulches, such as gravel for paths or pine needles under trees, make low-maintenance garden floors.

Creeping thyme (Thymus praecox) *forms a soft, fragrant carpet around stepping stones. This low-growing, drought-tolerant ground cover withstands light foot traffic.*

The Value of Ground Covers

The most valuable alternative to a lawn is the ground cover. A wide range of plants, including evergreen and deciduous woody shrubs, perennials, ornamental grasses, and even some vines, can serve as ground covers. All can grow fairly quickly into a dense blanket that covers the soil and suppresses weed growth. Some can even be walked upon like grass. And if you choose plants wisely and install them carefully, ground covers generally require less work than a lawn to maintain.

In addition, many ground covers will grow in difficult sites, such as shade, a steep bank, or very dry or moist soil, where lawns grow poorly if at all. And once established, most ground covers need fewer chemicals than either lawns or flower borders, requiring only an annual trimming and feeding to remain in good condition for years.

These practical advantages aside, ground covers can give new life and beauty to the garden. Low-growing ground covers, such as thyme *(Thymus serpyllum)* and woolly yarrow *(Achillea tomentosa)*, carpet the ground somewhat like grass but need only one mowing or trimming each year; they are lovely when grown around stepping stones. Spreading perennials planted in masses, including daylilies *(Hemerocallis* spp.), astilbes *(Astilbe* spp.), and creeping phlox *(P. stolonifera)*, produce showy flowers. A number of ground-covering shrubs have colorful fruits that decorate the garden in fall and winter—several cotoneaster species and creeping mahonia *(M. repens)* are popular examples. Some ground covers have subtle foliage, like the small gray leaves of lavender cotton *(Santolina chamaecyparissus)*; others, such as some of the hosta species, sport boldly variegated leaves. Textural contrasts between different ground covers and with adjacent lawns, patios, and paths also add further interest to the garden.

Versatile Vines

If lawns and ground covers are a garden's floors, then vines are often its walls. Flexible both in their manner of growth and in their varied uses in the landscape, vines can fill vertical space with leafy growth to screen unsightly vistas, clothe bare walls, cover unattractive fences, or soften the harsh lines of buildings. Many can be trained up and over arbors and pergolas to provide a shady and private retreat. Vines such as wisteria, the many sorts of clematis, and climbing roses offer beautiful and often fragrant flowers. Others, such as Boston ivy *(Parthenocissus tricuspidata)* and porcelain berry *(Ampelopsis brevipedunculata)*, feature colorful foliage or fruits in fall.

A number of vines can also fill horizontal space in the garden. They happily sprawl over the ground, quickly spreading into effective ground covers. Star jasmine *(Trachelospermum jasminoides)* and the memorial rose *(Rosa wichuraiana)* are good vines for covering banks or other large areas.

Whether you want to use vines as vertical plants or ground covers, choose a species suited to your climate and your purpose. Some vines are decidedly rampant growers, especially in milder climates, and need lots of space. Others are slower or grow with a more open pattern, making them less suitable for screening but good for training up a post. Check that as a vine climbs—whether it twines, clings by itself, holds by tendrils, or must be tied up—it fits with the support.

CHAPTER 1

Elements of Garden Design

*b*efore you even rent a rotary tiller or buy plants, you should give some thought to planning your garden. Spending some time preparing a good design will make the process of creating your landscape easier and more rewarding. It's a good idea to make a list of the components you would like to have in your garden, such as a play area, a shady retreat under an arbor, or a flower border. • Then make several rough drawings of the basic area, noting any desirable features that are already in place (such as trees and fences), as well as any problem spots (such as a steep bank or unsightly shed), where ground covers or vines might offer a solution. Now, sketch in different possible arrangements of the elements you want to add. • These steps will help you decide where you want lawnlike open spaces and where you might use vines to create a sense of privacy.

Planning Lawns

*T*he traditional garden design in America has been to plant a large area of lawn in both the front and back yards, install a patio next to the house, then plant a few shrubs and flowers around the patio, house, and lawn borders—almost as afterthoughts. A newer and more exciting approach is to first lay out the paths that will connect the important components of your garden to each other and also connect your home to the driveway and street. Then you can decide what to plant or build along and around the paths. Do you want a small lawn where children can play in one area, a patio made of pavers interplanted with creeping thyme in another area, and perhaps a mixed border of shrubs and small trees plus perennials and ground covers? This method of designing allows you to move away from thinking of a lawn as the necessary and inevitable central feature of the garden and results in more interesting and varied gardens that are also easier to maintain.

If you decide on a lawn area, there are several ways to reduce future maintenance chores while at the same time creating a pleasing design. To simplify mowing, avoid planting a lawn that extends into awkward corners. Also try to make any patches of lawn accessible to each other and to the mower's storage place. If there are trees in the lawn area, include wide basins around them to avoid nicking the bark with the mower and make mowing easier. Mowing will be even simpler if you group trees and shrubs in large beds and borders, with ground cover or mulch between them.

Another way to make future grass cutting easier is to install a mowing strip around any edges of the lawn that don't abut a hard surface, such as a patio. This strip, usually made of poured concrete or bricks laid on sand, provides a "roadway" for the mower's wheels, allowing the machine to trim the grass closely along the lawn's edges.

When designing a lawn area, think about future irrigation, too. If you will be watering with a hose-end sprinkler, avoid odd nooks and crannies that will require extra fussing with the sprinkler. Parking strips—the narrow area between the sidewalk and the street—often present maintenance problems when planted with grass; they are awkward both to irrigate and mow. Consider installing substantial stepping stones and a tough, low ground cover instead.

Finally, when deciding where you want to plant areas of lawn, be sure to consider the terrain and microclimates of your yard. You may find it easier to plant ground covers than grass in certain areas. If you have steep banks or hilly areas, for instance, it is difficult to establish a thick stand of lawn because grass seed tends to wash away down slopes and sod must be carefully pinned down lest it slip away. And mowing can be dangerous on hills, as mowers can tip over.

Banks are also tricky to irrigate—the water tends to run down the hill rather then soaking into the soil. Sides of the hills don't receive enough moisture, while poorly drained areas at the bases of hills or banks tend to remain waterlogged and are inhospitable to lawn grasses. It's usually necessary to install a drainage system before planting grass in such areas; planting ground-cover species that thrive in damp areas, such as creeping Jennie *(Lysimachia nummularia)* and many ferns, may be more practical.

Areas of deep shade under trees or close to the north side of buildings are also problematic for grass. Though some species will tolerate light shade, lawn grasses in general are sun-loving plants. There are many beautiful ground covers that thrive in the shade, however (see the sidebar on page 24).

This neatly edged lawn provides a tidy, quiet foreground
for a colorful border.

A small area of lawn con-
tributes a simple elegance to
this formal garden.

Lawn in a circular shape
gives a feeling of open space
and softens the edges of this
walled garden.

Guide to Lawn Grasses

Planting varieties of lawn grasses well suited both to your climate and to the intended use of your lawn will give you a good-looking and easy-to-maintain lawn. Research by seed companies and universities has led to the introduction of numerous improved cultivars of lawn grasses. Some are more resistant to insects and diseases than older cultivars; others are more tolerant of shade, drought, or heavy wear. Check with your county cooperative extension agent or local nurseries to find out about recent cultivars adapted to your area.

Lawn grasses are classified as either cool season or warm season. Cool-season grasses are generally adapted to northern climates, where they grow vigorously in spring and fall when daytime temperatures range from 60° to 75°F; in very hot summers they may turn brown. Cool-season grasses are often sold as a blend of several cultivars of the same species (for example, several cultivars of Kentucky bluegrass), or as a mixture of two or more different species (such as Kentucky bluegrass and fine fescue). Planting blends or mixtures is a good idea, because if one or more of the cultivars included is destroyed by disease or doesn't grow well in certain parts of your yard, chances are that others will take over and flourish. Below is a list of cool-season grasses with their advantages and unique features noted.

▼ *Fine fescue* is a general term for several species, including chewings fescue, hard fescue, and creeping red fescue, that are often found in mixtures with Kentucky bluegrass because they grow well in the shady areas of a lawn. They are also quite drought tolerant. In recent years, landscapers have planted hard fescue and creeping red fescue as low-maintenance ground covers on banks. As they grow to less than a foot in height, they can be left unmowed, giving a soft, rolling effect, like gentle waves.

▼ *Kentucky bluegrass* has been "king" of lawn grasses for generations because it produces a fine-textured deep green lawn. Some of the newer cultivars, such as 'Baron', 'Merit', and 'Ram I', require less water and fertilizer than older cultivars.

▼ *Perennial ryegrass* is an important component of cool-season grass mixes. It germinates quickly and produces a lawn that stands traffic better than Kentucky bluegrass. Newer cultivars, such as 'Palmer II', 'Repel II', 'Citation II', and a number of others, are also resistant to insects.

▼ *Tall fescue*, also known as turf-type tall fescue or dwarf tall fescue, is increasingly being recognized as a valuable lawn grass. Though older cultivars are coarse in appearance, over the past few years some 60 new cultivars have been introduced that have a finer

Kentucky bluegrass is the most widely planted cool-season grass, providing a lush, fine-textured lawn.

Perennial ryegrass, planted alone or in a mixture with other grasses, grows quickly and withstands traffic well.

texture and are also tolerant to drought, heat, and traffic; many resist damage from insects and diseases and grow in both sunny and shady areas.

In contrast to cool-season grasses, warm-season grasses are adapted to the South. They grow best during hot weather (80° to 90°F); most become dormant and brown when temperatures drop to freezing. The majority of these grasses spread by stolons (stems that run on the surface of the soil) or rhizomes (stems that run under the surface). The following warm-season grasses lend themselves to a variety of climatic conditions in the South.

▼ *Bahia grass* grows well in Florida and the Gulf states. It tolerates some drought but does better with abundant water. Bahia grass wears well and tends to stay green longer in winter than most other warm-season grasses.

▼ *Bermuda grass* is the most commonly planted grass in mild-winter West Coast and southern regions.

Bermuda grass falls into two general groups: those that can be started from seed (cultivars include 'Sundevil', 'Cheyenne', and 'Sahara') and a wider selection of hybrid cultivars that are grown from sod or sprigs. Both sorts of Bermuda grass tolerate drought and heat and also withstand traffic, but neither grows very happily in shade.

▼ *St. Augustine grass* is adapted to the humid coastal areas of the South. Most cultivars do not tolerate freezing temperatures. This aggressive grass has a coarse appearance but is adapted to both shade and sun and takes traffic.

▼ *Zoysia grass*, the most winter hardy of the southern grasses, grows best in the Upper South. It tolerates more shade than Bermuda grass but not as much as St. Augustine. Two cultivars, 'Meyer' and 'Emerald', are widely available. 'Emerald' has a finer leaf blade, while 'Meyer' can be somewhat more drought tolerant.

Flowering Lawns, Meadows, and Prairies

Prairie Grasses

Several grasses are basic to prairie gardens. Plant the taller ones if your garden receives more than 30 inches of rainfall a year; the shorter types are best in drier areas. Indian grass (Sorghastrum avenaceum) becomes a spectacular 5-foot fountain of long leaves with tall golden seed heads in fall. Big bluestem (Andropogon gerardii) forms a 6- to 10-foot column with rust-colored seed stems.

Little bluestem (Schizachyrium scoparium) usually grows 2 to 3 feet tall; its russet fall color accents the prairie well into winter. Very drought-tolerant shorter grasses include blue grama (Bouteloua gracilis), a 2-foot grass with fine-textured leaves; western wheatgrass (Agropyron smithii), which features distinctive blue leaves; and buffalo grass, described in the sidebar on page 15.

Many homeowners are taking a more relaxed approach to lawn care, allowing or encouraging low-growing flowering plants to mingle with the grass. This kind of lawn still requires mowing, though not as frequently as an all-grass lawn. Less fertilizer and irrigation will be needed, too. Some of the plants that add beauty and interest to a flowering lawn are English daisies *(Bellis perennis),* with tiny white or pink blooms; various yarrows *(Achillea spp.);* chamomile *(Chamaemelum spp.);* wild thyme *(Thymus serpyllum)*; and white clover *(Trifolium repens).* To create a flowering lawn, start from scratch, adding seeds of these plants to a grass seed mix, or overseed an existing lawn with these species. You can also transplant young plants directly into the grass.

In both meadows and prairies, bunchgrasses are the dominant plants, growing in association with many native wildflowers. These are interesting alternatives to lawns, requiring no fertilizer, little or no supplemental water, and only one mowing each year, once established. These plants aren't meant to be walked on, so it's necessary to design paths through a meadow or prairie planting.

In nature meadows occur where there is some summer rainfall, often in an opening in a wooded area. Besides grasses and wildflowers, sedges are often found in meadows, and there may be ferns and other shade-loving plants if the meadow merges into woods.

Only 150 years ago a vast sea of treeless grassland, called prairie by European settlers, covered the American heartland. Today prairies are being re-created by ecologists and homeowners. There are several different communities of prairie plants; the differences among these depend on annual rainfall and soil type. Tallgrass prairie existed in areas with higher rainfall (up to 40 inches a year) and somewhat richer soils. Farther west, the shortgrass prairie survived on as little as 20 inches of rainfall a year. There are, of course, many gradations in between these extremes.

To find out which native grasses and wildflowers would work best to create a meadow or prairie in your yard, check with your state's native plant society and native plant nurseries. Try to explore a nearby natural prairie or meadow where conditions are similar to your garden; arboretums and botanical gardens are excellent resources. It's a good idea to start with a basic list of two to four grasses and perhaps eight to a dozen wildflowers. As you learn more about local plants, you can add more species.

Avoid the meadow-in-a-can approach—these seed mixtures too often contain non-native and invasive species, as well as too many annual species of wildflowers that last only a year. Instead, buy seeds of individual species or, if available, container-grown plants that you can transplant.

In a mass planting, a swath of annual coreopsis (C. tinctoria) makes a natural and easy-to-maintain transition between the lawn and nearby woods.

Hardscape and Mulches

Garden designers use the term "hardscape" to refer to such nonliving features as patios, decks, and paths. In most cases these are fairly permanent and expensive structures, and their design and placement should be carefully considered.

The materials you choose for hardscaping will help set the overall style of your garden. Use materials that blend well with your house—for example, wooden decking suits a ranch-style house and brick seems more appropriate near a New England cottage. When choosing such materials as concrete pavers or flagstone, bring some samples home to see how they look in your yard before ordering. Combining materials, such as wooden railroad ties and paving slabs, can create an interesting and distinctive look. And for an inexpensive but durable surface, don't overlook recycled broken concrete chunks. After they are set in place, plant tiny spreaders like blue star creeper *(Laurentia fluviatilis)* or creeping thyme *(Thymus praecox)* between the pieces.

The outdoor room in many American gardens is often a single large patio or deck situated between the lawn and the back door. Designing, instead, several somewhat smaller patios or decks can give you more usable outdoor living space and at the same time reduce the amount of lawn or ground cover you must plant and maintain. Perhaps a smaller patio within sight of the house could hold a sandbox and a picnic table. Another patio, partially concealed by a vine-covered trellis, might serve as a tranquil area for outdoor tea parties; and if space permits, a third paved area, protected by a spreading tree or an arbor, could offer a shady retreat. You may want to unify the overall design by using similar materials for each surface and by connecting the outdoor rooms with paths made of the same or similar materials. Allowing plants to flow into the hardscape areas, disguising some of the hard edges, will also soften and integrate the design. For other ideas on combining hardscape and ground covers, see pages 20–22.

Mulches are used to suppress weeds and help the soil retain moisture. They are usually organic materials, like bark, but can also be gravel or small stones. Gravel, when properly installed (see page 65), can replace living ground covers or lawn around trees, as well as serving as a surface for paths. A layer of fir bark chunks, shredded bark, or tree chips under trees or large shrubs can make a nice path and soften the appearance of the landscape.

Bark mulch both defines and extends a stepping-stone path. The mulch also suppresses weed growth.

Paving stones accent the center of a garden of perennials and shrubs. Paths of the same material lead into the garden, unifying the scene and inviting exploration.

A soft gray flagstone floor fits well with the stone table and old wooden bench in this secluded nook.

Designing with Ground Covers

Tall Ground Covers

A number of taller plants can serve admirably as ground covers. Tall ground covers are especially useful in providing a natural transition from your garden to open space or woods beyond; massed plantings also provide cover for wildlife.

Some tall shrubs that work well in sunny areas include barberries (Berberis spp.) and tall species of cotoneaster pyracantha, and ceanothus. For shadier locations, groups of rhododendrons or azaleas are lovely.

Other ground-cover plants, such as daylilies (Hemerocallis spp.) and many ornamental grasses, grow tall when in bloom and either die back naturally to the ground or are cut back in late fall. This pattern of growth gives a varied appearance to the garden throughout the year.

A large-scale planting of foamflower (Tiarella cordifolia) *carpets a woodland area, creating a sweeping vista.*

Ground covers are a part of almost every well-designed garden, helping to unify the diverse plants in the landscape. For example, a background planting of two or three different trees plus a clutch of flowering shrubs seems less cluttered if tied together by an underplanting of a single ground cover, such as creeping cotoneaster *(C. adpressus)*.

Ground covers provide a visual link between trees and shrubs and the earth. You can think of plantings as layers that range from the tallest trees down to plants that hug the ground. You might use a 1- to 3-foot-high ground cover, such as creeping mahonia

(M. repens), to connect taller shrubs with a lower ground cover, such as bishop's hat *(Epimedium grandiflorum)*.

Ground covers can also provide a smooth transition from your garden to the nearby natural environment, whether this is a wood or a rolling hillside. Native plants make good bridging ground covers: For shade, try wintergreen *(Gaultheria procumbens)*, ferns, or partridgeberry *(Mitchella repens)*; for sunny areas, bearberry *(Arctostaphylos spp.)*, dwarf coyote brush *(Baccharis pilularis)*, or various ceanothus species. Planting the same ground cover in several areas of your garden also helps unify the whole.

Haircap moss (Polytrichum spp.) *and wintergreen* (Gaultheria procumbens), *a native evergreen ground cover, contrast pleasantly in dappled shade.*

Foamflower (Tiarella poly-phylla) *is an effective bloom-ing ground cover for moist soil in the shade of tall trees—conditions that don't suit lawn grasses.*

Succulent ground covers, such as this sedum (S. kamt-schaticum) *shown above, flow naturally around rocks and boulders in sunny areas.*

Designing with Ground Covers

**TROUBLESHOOTING
TIP**

When choosing ground covers for shady areas, keep in mind the various levels of shade, which range from dappled light under high-branching trees to dense shade under large conifers. Also, plants that grow well in full sun in cooler northern climates are often good candidates for light shade in the hot, humid South.

Many ground covers work well around large rocks, boulders, and rocky outcroppings on your property. A planting of hen-and-chickens *(Sempervivum tectorum)* sets off rocks perfectly, as do the red-tinged foliage and red flowers of *Sedum spurium* 'Dragon's Blood'. On a large scale, natural plantings can feature woody ground covers spreading around and over rocks, such as a combination of ceanothus *(C. gloriosus)* with California sagebrush *(Artemisia californica* 'Canyon Gray'). Ornamental grasses are also beautiful with large rocks, especially when combined with tall salvia species or perennial sunflowers *(Helianthus × multiflorus)*.

Ground covers also help make decks and patios into integral parts of the garden without a lot of extra maintenance. Use ground covers with interesting foliage to soften the edges of human-made structures, at the same time settling such structures into the garden in a natural way. Planning cutouts—unpaved

The lustrous green leaves of carpet bugleweed (Ajuga reptans) *soften the edges of a small patio and tie together the rest of the planting (hostas, coralbells, and a Japanese maple).*

squares or sections—in a patio breaks up the expanse of paving and gives you a place for such ground covers as ornamental grasses or sedums; this treatment also makes the pavement seem cooler on a hot day.

A number of evergreen plants provide handsome edgings or low borders for decks and patios. In partial shade, sweet violet *(Viola odorata)* emanates its romantic fragrance in spring. In mild-winter climates, star jasmine *(Trachelospermum jasminoides)* is a beautiful and fragrant choice for a larger-scale evergreen edging near seating areas. Germander *(Teucrium chamaedrys)* also makes a tidy edging, while lamb's-ears *(Stachys byzantina)* gives a more casual effect.

Decks or patios on hillsides often have retaining walls. Try softening these with evergreen ground covers that drape or trail, such as creeping rosemary *(Rosmarinus officinalis* 'Prostratus') for warm climates or a small cotoneaster, such as *C. microphyllus*. Wall rock cress *(Arabis caucasica)* and sun rose *(Helianthemum nummularium)* are good for draping and offer showy spring flowers.

Open space, whether a patio, deck, or lawn, is a necessary part of a garden. Ground covers help define the edges of open spaces—for example, a line of blue fescue *(Festuca ovina* var. *glauca)* delineates a patio from a flower border. Or ground covers can be used to carpet open spaces. Very low plants that grow horizontally or flat on the ground are best for this purpose, such as creeping thyme *(Thymus praecox)*, English ivy *(Hedera helix)*, one of the prostrate junipers *(Juniperus horizontalis* or *J. conferta)*, or bearberry. These low-growing ground covers also emphasize the natural terrain of your garden; they are especially effective on sloping ground or banks.

Ornamental Grasses as Ground Covers

Ornamental Grasses to Choose

A few ornamental grasses grow well in shade, but others need full sun to flourish. In shade try tufted hair grass (Deschampsia caespitosa); it's an excellent ground cover for moist areas. Dense tufts of dark green foliage grow 1 to 4 feet tall; the showy flowering stalks appear in late May. Snowy wood rush (Luzula nivea) is not a true grass but a member of the rush family. It features showy white flowers in late spring. This plant prefers moist shade but also grows well in dry shaded locations.

Most of the prairie grasses described on page 16 are good choices for ground cover in sunny areas. Deer grass (Muhlenbergia rigens) is well suited to western gardens with little rainfall. This native grass forms dense clumps 2 to 3 feet tall with flower stalks rising to 5 feet. Another western native, purple needlegrass (Stipa pulchra), is smaller at about 1½ feet tall and is effective planted in large groups. Its flower stalks emerge in April, giving a soft, feathery purple cast to the planting.

*A*merican gardeners are increasingly using ornamental grasses in their gardens. Ornamental grasses are valued for their interesting colors and textures and the gentle movement of their leaves and flowering stems (or culms) in the wind. Some grasses, such as most forms of *Miscanthus* and pampas grass *(Cortaderia selloana)*, grow too large to serve as ground covers. Many others, however, are excellent candidates. Groups of a single species of an ornamental grass can give your landscape a feeling of elegant simplicity.

Plantings of feather reed grass (*Calamagrostis acutiflora* var. *stricta*) or one of the fountain grasses (*Pennisetum alopecuroides* or *P. orientale*) provide gracefully arching clumps of leaves, topped by flowering culms that add gentle height in summer and fall. A large clump of Japanese blood grass (*Imperata cylindrica* 'Red Baron') is stunning in late summer, when the leaves turn a deep red; use it to set off a quieter planting of prostrate blue junipers (*Juniperus* spp.). Blue fescue (*Festuca ovina* var. *glauca*) offers a dense, rounded mound of bluish foliage. Try it along a path or arranged in a geometric pattern. Or group blue fescue next to snow-in-summer (*Cerastium tomentosum*) or lamb's-ears (*Stachys byzantina*).

Some ornamental grasses recommended as ground covers should be treated with caution because they spread aggressively and are likely to invade other plantings. Blue lyme grass (*Elymus arenarius* 'Glaucus') is effective for erosion control on coastal

A variegated form of dwarf lilyturf (Liriope muscari) *makes an attractive evergreen ground cover between a path and a fence. The lilac flower spikes are a bonus in summer.*

bluffs, but in the garden it should be placed in a drainage tile or surrounded by concrete to contain its wandering rhizomes. Ribbon grass (*Phalaris arundinacea* var. *picta*) has beautifully striped foliage. It can be a valuable ground cover for areas with poor soil but spreads too fast in regular garden soil. The cultivar 'Dwarf Garters' is less aggressive.

Ground Covers in Difficult Locations

Shade-Tolerant Ground Covers

Shrubby ground covers for shade include the elegant evergreen spreading English yew (Taxus baccata 'Repandens'), the evergreen blackberry relative Rubus calycinoides, and deciduous bunchberry (Cornus canadensis).

For flowering ground covers in light shade and moist soil, plant a spreading perennial, such as dwarf Chinese astilbe (A. chinensis 'Pumila'), which has fluffy pink flowers, or the lungworts (Pulmonaria spp.), which sport beautifully speckled foliage and flowers in blue, violet, red, or white.

Lilyturf (Liriope or Ophiopogon spp.) gives a clumping grasslike effect, while Irish moss (Arenaria spp.) and Scotch moss (Sagina spp.), as well as many native mosses, form soft green carpets in shade.

*B*esides adding beauty and interest, ground covers can solve garden problems. So many different plants can serve as ground covers that you can find some to grow in even the most difficult spots.

Shady areas are often especially problematic. Most lawn grasses sulk in the shade, and many familiar flowering plants are unhappy, too. However, dozens of ground-cover plants are adapted to shade, and many look wonderful combined with each other. For example, ferns are lovely with one of the wild gingers *(Asarum canadense, A. caudatum,* or *A. europaeum),* epimediums, and many hostas. Let carpet bugleweed *(Ajuga reptans)* spread around sweet box *(Sarcococca hookerana* var. *humilis)* for a long-lasting cover.

When planting ground covers in the shade, try some new versions of old favorites. Even the standby Japanese spurge *(Pachysandra terminalis)* is available

in a more interesting variegated form as well as in a deep green cultivar, 'Green Carpet'. The native Alleghany pachysandra *(P. procumbens)* is a more disease-resistant choice for warmer regions of the Southeast.

Hillsides and banks are also areas that can be inhospitable to lawn. In such situations, try a cotoneaster species, which looks beautiful flowing over a sunny bank. Besides shiny leaves, cotoneasters feature small white or pink flowers in spring and showy red berries in fall. The many ground-covering junipers *(Juniperus* spp.*)* are also well adapted to hot, sunny banks and hillsides; their foliage color ranges from gray blue to silver to green tipped with gold.

English ivy *(Hedera helix),* the more frost-tender Algerian ivy *(H. canariensis),* and vinca *(V. major)* are tough ground covers for sunny or shady banks, as is

Vinca makes a sturdy, versatile ground cover for large areas, city gardens, and sunny or shady spots. Its trailing shoots root as they spread.

Many-rooted English ivy (Hedera helix) effectively controls erosion on a bank that's too steep for lawn, and it tolerates more shade than many other ground covers.

Moss pink (Phlox subulata) *is a good ground cover for rock gardens and slopes. Its brilliant flowers appear in late spring.*

Drought-tolerant ground covers for southwestern gardens include cacti and blanket flower (Gaillardia × grandiflora).

Aaron's-beard *(Hypericum calycinum).* These sturdy ground covers can all be very aggressive, so plant them only where there is enough space.

Some of the tough, shrubby ground covers recommended for banks are also very tolerant of drought, especially junipers, cotoneasters, and Aaron's-beard. In the arid West, low-growing native shrubs are masters at surviving long, dry summers; in fact, most will die if overwatered in summer. These include ceanothus species, dwarf coyote brush *(Baccharis pilularis),* and bearberries *(Arctostaphylos* spp.*).* A highly drought-tolerant import from the Mediterranean, rock rose *(Cistus salviifolius),* is covered with white flowers in late spring to early summer.

By contrast, some gardens have poorly drained areas that remain damp all year. Very low-growing ground covers for damp (but not truly swampy) areas include baby's-tears *(Soleirolia soleirolii);* Corsican mint *(Mentha requinii),* whose tiny leaves emit a pleasant minty fragrance when crushed; and creeping Jennie *(Lysimachia nummularia)*—the golden-leaved form, *L. m.* 'Aurea', is especially pretty in light shade. Chameleon plant *(Houttuynia cordata* 'Chameleon'*)* grows to 9 inches high and its 3-inch-long leaves are splashed rather gaudily with green, yellow, and red. The perennial forget-me-not *(Myosotis scorpioides)* is known for its flowers of purest light blue borne on spreading plants only 3 to 6 inches high. Many ferns are also happy in damp, shady spots, as are the grasslike plants in the *Carex* genus.

Drought-Tolerant Ground Covers

Some of the prettiest water-thrifty ground covers come from herb gardens. Grouping several of these species can make charming ground-cover combinations for full sun. Woolly yarrow (Achillea tomentosa) forms a flat, dense mat of furry leaves, topped in summer with clusters of yellow flowers. There are a number of mat-forming thymes that look great planted near lamb's-ears (Stachys byzantina) or catmint (Nepeta × faassenii). Creeping rosemary (Rosmarinus officinalis 'Prostratus') drapes beautifully over banks or walls and features blue flowers. The small, evergreen shrubby santolinas (Santolina chamaecyparissus and S. virens) are effective when intermingled in drifts.

Other Uses for Ground Covers

Ground covers, such as the sweet woodruff (Galium odoratum) *shown here, combine charmingly with spring bulbs. Later, the ground cover will hide the yellow, ripened foliage of the bulbs.*

Creeping ground covers with tiny leaves and flowers look charming carpeting the ground around stepping stones in a path. Many also flourish growing out of cracks in pavement, where they crowd out weeds. Baby's-tears *(Soleirolia soleirolii)*, Corsican mint *(Mentha requienii)*, and creeping Jennie *(Lysimachia nummularia)* all do well in fairly shady, moist places, while woolly yarrow *(Achillea tomentosa)*, creeping thyme *(Thymus praecox)*, and chamomile *(Chamaemelum nobile)* are ideal for sunny areas. For either sun or light shade, try creeping speedwell *(Veronica repens)*, which grows 2 to 4 inches high and produces beautiful blue flowers in late spring, or blue star creeper *(Laurentia fluviatilis)*, a delightful little plant with starry light blue flowers in spring.

Besides carpeting paths around stepping stones, these low ground covers can function as alternatives to lawn when planted in larger areas. They offer a tidy, uniform surface, similar in feeling to turf, but require much less frequent mowing, growing denser and looking their best when mowed once or twice a year. Most, however, can take only very limited foot traffic; see the sidebar on page 27 for a few lawn substitutes that survive more wear.

Another good use for ground covers is to conceal messy, aging bulb foliage and also add interest to the overall design. By planting either evergreens or deciduous ground covers that develop leaves in mid- to late spring, you can delight in spring-flowering bulbs but minimize the distraction of their foliage, which must remain on the plant, ripening and turning brown, if the bulbs are to bloom again.

Bulbs, in turn, can enliven ground covers. Punctuate a wide ruff of periwinkle *(Vinca minor)* around a deciduous tree with tall-growing daffodils—this is most effective if you choose a periwinkle with variegated leaves. Daffodils or snowdrops also make commonplace ground covers, such as ivy or pachysandra, more appealing. A combination of leadwort *(Ceratostigma plumbaginoides)* and grape hyacinths *(Muscari spp.)* gives a long show, with the bulbs flowering in early spring and the leadwort offering cobalt blue blossoms in summer and bronze foliage in fall.

Aromatic Roman chamomile (Chamaemelum nobile) *makes a unique cushion for a stone bench.*

Blue star creeper (Laurentia fluviatilis) *fills the cracks between sections of a garden path, helping the path blend into the surrounding beds.*

In areas of high fire danger, ground covers serve a different function. By planting fire-retardant ground-cover species (including lawn) in a 50-foot band around structures and avoiding highly flammable trees and larger shrubs that can create "fire ladders" into trees, gardeners can maintain safer landscapes that are also attractive. Low-growing plants with a high moisture content, such as sedums and many of the ground covers lumped together under the common name "ice plant" (including *Delosperma alba, Drosanthemum floribundum,* and *Lampranthus* spp.) are excellent choices. African daisy *(Arctotheca calendula),* woolly yarrow, low-growing rock roses such as *Cistus salviifolius,* creeping rosemary *(Rosmarinus officinalis* 'Prostratus'), santolina, germander *(Teucrium* spp.), and the lawn substitute frogfruit *(Phyla nodiflora)* are all recommended.

Ground Covers That Withstand Traffic

Several interesting lawn substitutes will take some traffic. Chamomile (Chamaemelum nobile) forms a low, dense mat of finely divided bright evergreen leaves with small yellow or white flowers. Mow after flowering to keep neat. 'Treneague', a non-flowering cultivar, stays low without mowing.

Dichondra micrantha is a beautiful lawn substitute where winter temperatures stay above 25°F. It requires plenty of water and is susceptible to several pests.

Frogfruit (Phyla nodiflora), zones 9 to 10, is well adapted to heat and survives with little water but looks better with regular irrigation. The creeping stems have small, oval, gray-green leaves and lavender flowers that attract bees.

Irish moss (Arenaria verna) and Scotch moss (Sagina subulata), zones 5 to 10, cover small areas with a soft, velvetlike carpet. Plant in rich, moist soil in sun in cool climates (give afternoon shade in warmer areas).

Design Qualities of Ground Covers

Ground Covers with Variegated Foliage

Hostas offer some of the most dramatic variegated leaves, blending wonderfully with smaller ground covers, such as periwinkle. Spotted dead nettle (Lamium maculatum) offers some choice selections with silver-and-green leaves that look wonderful under flowering shrubs. One cultivar, 'Beacon Silver', has pink flowers; another, 'White Nancy', has white flowers.

Lilyturf (Liriope muscari), a ground cover frequently used in the shade of trees and shrubs and along walks in the humid Southeast, is available in several handsome variegated forms, including 'Silvery Sunproof' and 'Variegata'.

Some of the variegated grasses and sedges are also excellent as ground covers. Variegated Japanese sedge (Carex morrowii 'Variegata'), a good ground cover for shade, grows up to 1½ feet tall; its stiff green leaves have a lustrous silver margin. Another good shade plant is variegated moor grass (Molina caerula 'Variegata'), which has 16-inch-long green leaves, each with a distinct light cream stripe.

*B*esides choosing ground-cover species that are suited for your climate and the job you want them to perform in your landscape, consider the color and texture of the plants.

We often think of color in plants in terms of flower color, but flowers are only a fleeting occurrence in most plants, while foliage lasts for most or all of the year. Even "green" foliage color varies considerably, ranging from yellowish to bluish to gray. The leaves of most ground-cover plants fall somewhere in the middle of this spectrum. Plants with a yellow-green cast to their leaves include some hostas and junipers, golden thyme (*Thymus × citriodorus* 'Aureus'), and the golden form of creeping Jennie (*Lysimachia nummularia* 'Aurea'). On the other end of the green spectrum, plants with blue-green foliage include some hostas and junipers; grays are represented by lamb's-ears (*Stachys byzantina*), lavender cotton (*Santolina chamaecyparissus*), blue fescue (*Festuca ovina* var. *glauca*), snow-in-summer (*Cerastium tomentosum*), and woolly yarrow (*Achillea tomentosa*). Keep in mind that cool blue and gray tones will seem to recede in the landscape, creating an illusion of greater space, while warmer yellow colors will come forward and reduce distances.

Ground-cover plants with red or purple leaves can add a dramatic and unusual touch to the landscape. A few to consider are *Ajuga reptans* 'Purpurea' and *A. pyramidalis* 'Metallica Crispa' and purple alumroot (*Heuchera micrantha* 'Palace Purple'). Barberries offer two beautifully colored cultivars, *Berberis thunbergii* 'Crimson Pygmy' and *B. t.* 'Rose Glow'.

Ground-cover plants with variegated foliage bring color and contrast that last for many months in the garden. Many variegated plants are adapted to shade—in fact, their foliage may burn in hot sun.

Choosing variegated forms of the more common ground covers, such as Japanese spurge (*Pachysandra terminalis* 'Variegata') and periwinkle (*Vinca major* 'Variegata'), can make a planting much more interesting. Beautifully variegated forms of wintercreeper (*Euonymus fortunei*) and cotoneaster are also available to liven up a "typical" planting.

The texture of each ground cover's leaves, as well as stem buds and bark, should be considered along with foliage color. Textures range from fine and airy to coarse and dense; texture also varies with the reflective qualities of a plant's leaves—some are shiny, others dull or fuzzy. Combining fine-textured ferns with wide-leaved hostas and smaller-leaved pachysandras is more interesting than planting just one species.

One of the most colorful variegated ground covers is chameleon plant (Houttuynia cordata 'Chameleon'), a vigorous spreader in damp soil.

The shiny leaves of European wild ginger (Asarum europaeum) *bring glints of light to shady areas.*

Lamb's-ears (Stachys byzantina) *has thick, fuzzy leaves; the cultivar 'Silver Carpet' has extra-dense foliage and doesn't flower.*

The large leaves of mayapple (Podophyllum peltatum), *a North American native, carpet the floor of a damp woodland.*

The lacy fronds of ferns make a delicate ground cover for shade. Shown here is Adiantum venustum.

Substituting another fine-textured plant, such as astilbe, for the ferns, or substituting sweet woodruff *(Galium odoratum)* for the Japanese spurge, is a variation on this theme. Swaths of juniper and English ivy *(Hedera helix)* set off the texture of each plant, as does a combination of rockspray cotoneaster *(C. horizontalis)* and Scotch heather *(Calluna vulgaris)*; these plantings might be further enriched with groups of strap-leaved daylilies *(Hemerocallis spp.)*, lily-of-the-Nile *(Agapanthus africanus)*, or an ornamental grass.

Some ground covers are noted for their showy flowers; often these are planted in large swaths to make a bright picture that lasts for several weeks or longer, after which their reliable foliage takes over. In climates with mild winters, trailing African daisy *(Osteospermum fruticosum)* flowers in purple and white throughout the winter months. The various "ice plants" glow with vivid pink, purple, and red daisylike flowers in winter or spring. Trailing lantana *(L. montevidensis)* provides clusters of rosy purple flowers for much of the year.

In colder climates, creeping phlox *(P. stolonifera)* brings shady woodlands to life in spring with soft lavender-blue flowers. The related moss pink *(Phlox subulata)* is known for becoming a bright floral carpet of white, pink, or lavender in early summer. This plant makes a good edging or a cover for sunny banks. And lily-of-the-valley *(Convallaria majalis)* is popular because of its fragrant white flowers, but its 8-inch blue-green leaves are also attractive after the flowers fade. This tough, spreading (sometimes invasive) ground cover has the advantage of growing well in light to deep shade.

Vines for Screening and Shading

How Vines Climb

Learning how different vines climb will help you decide which kind of support each needs.

Some vines, such as English ivy (Hedera helix), *climbing fig* (Ficus pumila), *and climbing hydrangea* (Hydrangea anomala *subsp.* petiolaris), *climb by means of aerial roots or holdfasts; they can attach themselves directly to solid walls, fences, and tree trunks.*

Other vines, such as honeysuckle (Lonicera spp.), *morning-glory* (Ipomoea tricolor), *and wisteria species, hoist themselves aloft by twining their stems around supports such as wires or lattices.*

Still other vines climb by twisting tendrils or leaf stems around a slender support, such as a wire. Grapes, clematis, and passionflower (Passiflora spp.) *all grow in this manner.*

Some plants grown as vines, including climbing roses (Rosa hybrids) *and bougainvillea* (B. × buttiana), *have arching stems that need to be tied to a support to encourage them to grow upward; otherwise they will sprawl on the ground.*

Vines are versatile plants that can quickly provide a living screen to give you privacy from neighbors or nearby roads and to hide unsightly storage areas.

For screening purposes, grow climbers (vines that either twine or hold on with tendrils) on lattice panels set in a wooden frame supported by strong posts. A similar frame fitted with strong wire mesh or with vertical wires fixed every 6 inches with eye bolts will also work for such vines. Climbers include many of the honeysuckles; these are evergreen in mild-winter climates but lose their leaves in winter in colder regions. Trumpet honeysuckle (*Lonicera sempervirens*) and goldflame honeysuckle (*L. × heckrottii* 'Goldflame') are two attractive choices. Some of the more vigorous clematis species also make excellent screens. Deciduous anemone clematis (*C. montana*) gives a massive display of pink to white flowers in spring on vigorous 20-foot vines. Evergreen clematis (*C. armandii*) forms a substantial screen covered with fragrant white flowers in spring.

Vines can help add height to an existing fence, increasing the privacy of your home and garden. Fasten lightweight trellis panels to the top of the fence, or extend the posts upward a foot or two and attach strong galvanized wire between them. Planting vines to climb both the fence and the upward extensions will tie these structural materials together. Evergreen English ivy (*Hedera helix*) is one good choice for such a situation.

The cultivar of morning-glory (Ipomoea tricolor) *called 'Heavenly Blue' lives up to its name, blooming with rich color on a fast-growing annual vine.*

The flaming orange-red flowers of trumpet creeper (Campsis radicans) *grow prolifically on a tall-growing vine, which quickly covers a porch or arbor.*

Overhead structures, such as a simple trellis over a deck or patio, an arbor, or an ornate pergola set as a focal point in the garden, will give you privacy from uphill neighbors. Vines enhance all of these structures by softening their outlines, as well as tying them to the earth and to other plantings.

Growing vines on overhead structures is also the fastest way to create a leafy shaded area in a new or treeless garden. Often deciduous vines are a good choice for this job, providing needed shade in summer but letting in sunlight and warmth in winter. On large overhead structures, wisteria works well for both shade and privacy. These vines are better able to twine around large-diameter posts than most other vines, and their drooping flower clusters look beautiful from a seat below on a deck or patio.

Grapes *(Vitis* spp.*)* and arbors go well together, making an idyllic retreat complete with delicious fruit in fall. Ask a local nursery about varieties that are well suited to your area. Grape vines are deciduous and grow quickly; although they have tendrils, the vines need to be trained and tied to their supports.

Porches, by definition, already have a roof to provide shade, but they are enhanced by vines. Training vines on wires so that they drape over the eaves of the porch roof, or on a trellis to shade the porch's open sides, can create a cool and shady retreat from the heat of summer. Fast-growing Dutchman's-pipe *(Aristolochia durior)*, a twining vine with large, glossy, kidney-shaped leaves, will cover such a trellis in one season. Sweet autumn clematis *(C. paniculata)* or, in mild-winter regions, one of the jasmines *(Jasminum spp.)* will produce fragrant flowers that are especially welcome near a porch.

Vines for Camouflage

Knowing which way a vine twines makes it easier to train. Vines that twine from left to right (clockwise) include hardy kiwi (Actinidia arguta) *and other* Actinidia *species; Dutchman's-pipe* (Aristolochia durior), *bittersweet* (Celastrus spp.), *and Chinese wisteria* (W. sinensis). *Counterclockwise twiners include some of the honeysuckles* (Lonicera spp.), *Chinese magnolia vine* (Schisandra chinensis), *and Japanese wisteria* (W. floribunda).

*B*esides screening views into or out of the garden, vines can camouflage unsightly garages and sheds and soften the appearance of chain-link fences and brick, concrete, or wooden walls and fences.

When choosing vines for these purposes, it is important to know the eventual size of the mature vine and how it climbs. For example, silver lace vine *(Polygonum aubertii)* or American bittersweet *(Celastrus scandens)* will quickly produce a dense cover over a shed or a fence, but neither will stop there; they will move on to take over all nearby territory, too. Slightly less vigorous vines, perhaps anemone clematis *(C. montana* 'Alba'*)* or Dutchman's-pipe *(Aristolochia durior)*, perform the same function in the landscape but are somewhat easier to control.

Vines that cling with aerial roots ("holdfasts"), such as Boston ivy *(Parthenocissus tricuspidata)*, trumpet creeper *(Campsis radicans)*, and English ivy *(Hedera helix)*, will clamber up any surface. They shouldn't, however, be used on wood shingles because they can work their way into small crevices, forcing the shingles apart. Aerial roots also damage the surface of smooth wooden walls and are difficult to remove before painting.

Vines that cling *are* a good choice for brick, stucco, and concrete, as long as they can be kept away from wooden window and door frames. For evergreen vines to cover a masonry wall that faces north or east, try English ivy or wintercreeper *(Euonymus fortunei)*. In the North these vines may be burned by winter cold if planted on the south or west side of a house or wall, where the afternoon sun dries out the leaves.

A climbing rose (Rosa 'New Dawn') *trained on a wooden trellis decorates a blank wall and provides a pretty backdrop for a perennial border.*

Use vigorous vines, such as wisteria, to camouflage unsightly tree trunks. The vine shown here is a double-flowered form, Wisteria sinensis 'Plena'.

Grape vines grow happily intertwined with Virginia creeper (Parthenocissus quinquefolia). Here the plants conceal the wire fence and give privacy.

Deciduous clinging vines for masonry include Boston ivy, whose cultivar 'Veitchii' has smaller leaves that are purple when young. The related silver vein creeper *(Parthenocissus henryana)* has exceptionally beautiful leaves on a less vigorous vine. Climbing hydrangea *(H. anomala* subsp. *petiolaris)* is slow to start but eventually becomes very large; its beautiful wide flower clusters are worth the wait. Like silver vein creeper, it grows best in partial shade.

Vines that climb with tendrils or by twining on trellis or wire are best to cover wooden house walls and fences. Choices include five-leaf akebia *(Akebia quinata)*, honeysuckles *(Lonicera* spp.), wisteria, and for mild-winter climates, jasmines.

Chain-link fences usually need some embellishment, and vines that twine or hold on with tendrils are easy to establish on this ready-made support. Anemone clematis *(C. montana* 'Alba'), honeysuckles, or star jasmine *(Trachelospermum jasminoides)* can turn such a fence into a beautiful "hedge." Clinging vines, like

English ivy and wintercreeper, will also grow on chain link, making fairly flat vertical surfaces. All vines need occasional shearing to keep them in bounds, especially if the fence is near a walkway.

Annual vines can quickly provide camouflage or add visual interest to fences and walls; they are also useful to fill in while slower-growing vines are getting under way. Scarlet runner bean *(Phaseolus coccineus)* flowers in scarlet on vines that twine to 5 feet in height; the beans are edible if picked while young. Hyacinth bean *(Dolichos lablab)* has a similar growth pattern, and its purplish leaves set off by white, pink, or purple flowers are even more decorative. Morningglory *(Ipomoea tricolor)* blooms later in summer; the best-known cultivar is the aptly named 'Heavenly Blue', but other colors are available. The familiar trailing nasturtium *(Tropaeolum majus)* makes a quick, bright cover that tolerates sun and some drought.

Vines for Quick Cover

The genus Actinidia *(one species of which produces the popular kiwifruit) offers several interesting and fast-growing deciduous twining vines. The hardy kiwi (A. arguta) grows to 30 feet and has lustrous green, oval leaves up to 6 inches long. To produce the small non-fuzzy fruits called Chinese gooseberries, it is usually necessary to plant both female and male vines, though there is a self-fertile cultivar, 'Issai'. Kolomikta actinidia (A. kolomikta) is smaller, to 20 feet, and has unique foliage variegated with white or pink.*

Cross vine (Bignonia capreolata) *is one of the hardiest evergreen flowering vines for year-round cover. It can grow to 50 feet and has 2-inch reddish orange flowers.*

Trumpet creeper (Campsis radicans), *native to the eastern United States, is a tall, vigorous clinger with showy orange-scarlet flowers in midsummer to early fall. It makes a quick cover.*

Vines as Architectural Elements

A vine-covered fence provides a simple dark green background for a bed of lilies (Lilium spp.) and daylilies (Hemerocallis spp.).

Most gardens are strongly horizontal, featuring level lawns, ground covers, patios, or decks. Vines trained on supports can add a much-needed vertical accent, while taking up relatively little ground space.

A vine-covered arch, freestanding or built over a gate, clearly marks the entrance to the garden, or it can serve as a transition between two parts of the property. Place arches so that they frame the view of the area beyond, perhaps leading the eye to a focal point, such as a small pond or a special plant.

On a larger scale, an arbor—basically a larger arch—can be sited to lead directly to another part of the garden. Or an arbor can serve to partially mask a section of the garden, making the area beyond seem somewhat mysterious, a place to be explored. You can also set up an arbor as a destination or as a restful place at the end of a garden path.

In all these cases, vines help make the structure a living part of the garden. And the climber you choose greatly influences the overall effect of the structure. Planting airy, open vines, such as a hybrid clematis or porcelain berry *(Ampelopsis brevipedunculata)*, reinforces the feeling of looking through and beyond the arch or arbor. Heavier vines with a dense habit of growth, such as grapes *(Vitis* spp.*)* or kiwi *(Actinidia* spp.*)*, limit the view beyond and give the structure a stronger presence.

Climbers can introduce a vertical element in other ways, too. Pillars, ranging from simple posts to open wrought-iron structures to Grecian-style columns, can be used to frame a view or provide a strong vertical point in a flower bed. Solid pillars need a wrapping of wire to give twining vines something to hold onto; the stems of nontwining vines, such as climbing roses, can

Climbing on a trellis, these pale-flowered roses ('White Cap' and 'City of York') divide the garden without completely blocking the view of the area beyond.

be tucked into the wire as they grow. A simple tripod, made of three stakes held together at the top with wire or twine, serves much the same purpose but in a more casual, natural style. *Lonicera × heckrottii* 'Goldflame', an open-growing smaller hybrid honeysuckle with intriguing flowers that are a rich purple-pink outside and yellow inside, looks good on a tripod, as do any number of annual vines, including scarlet runner beans *(Phaseolus coccineus)*, sweet peas *(Lathyrus odoratus)*, and decorative gourds *(Cucurbita pepo* var. *overifera* and *Lagenaria siceraria).*

Vines grown on fences or screens make a pleasing backdrop for a flower border, giving it a stronger vertical dimension and providing a bit of shade and protection from wind, both of which are helpful to flowering plants. Best of all, you can choose climbers to enhance the overall design. If the flower bed is colorful, use vines grown primarily for foliage as a calming green background. Miniature grape ivy *(Cissus striata)*, hardy outdoors in zones 9 and 10, is an evergreen vine with glossy, divided foliage that makes an elegant background. English ivy *(Hedera helix)*, especially a smaller-leaved variant such as 'Baltica', has a similar effect.

Flowering vines planted as a backdrop can add to the overall color scheme and give the garden a feeling of abundance. Use golden clematis *(C. tangutica)*, with its nodding, bell-shaped yellow flowers, to complement the blue and purple asters of late summer and fall. Large-flowered clematis hybrids come in many beautiful tones of pink, purple, white, mauve, and red, and will work in any garden composition.

Trellises

Vines for Trellises

Vines that twine or form tendrils grow well on trellises. Consider Clematis × jackmanii, *a fairly vigorous vine with large purple-blue flowers; there are cultivars with blue, red, or violet blossoms, too. The evergreen leaves of Carolina yellow jessamine* (Gelsemium sempervirens) *form a delicate green curtain on a trellis, highlighted by fragrant yellow flowers in late winter to early spring. Potato vine* (Solanum jasminoides), *evergreen in the mildest winters, blooms practically all year with a froth of bluish white flowers.*

Downy clematis (C. macropetala) *is somewhat smaller than most other clematis, growing 6 to 10 feet tall; its lavender to powder blue flowers appear in early spring. Scarlet clematis* (C. texensis) *is also smaller, growing to 10 feet or so, and is more tolerant of dry soil than other clematis.*

Vines and climbing plants can be trained on trellises that are either fastened to a permanent wall or freestanding. It's easier to make a sturdy trellis if you attach it to a building wall or to a strong fence. To carry the weight of a heavy vine—and most vines are heavy—support a freestanding trellis between strong posts set in concrete. Save smaller, lightweight trellises for more delicate vines.

Materials for trellises run the gamut from simple and rustic to elegant. Trellises for deciduous vines

Several large-flowered hybrid clematis twine about an iron standard, making an interesting vertical accent.

need to be attractive in their own right, as they will be bare of foliage for part of the year.

Wire, either single strands fastened to a frame or field fencing, is probably the least expensive trellis and works well for dense vines that will hide the wire. Be careful about using wire in very sunny areas, as hot metal will burn the stems or tendrils of young vines. Recycled reinforcing bars can be bent into interesting free-form trellises (this requires strong arms) or fastened in a grid to a fence. Many sorts of wrought-iron trellises are available and can be installed next to a wall or as freestanding structures in your garden. Natural materials to fashion into trellises include flexible willow stems, grape vines, and bamboo.

Trellises made from milled lumber include lattice, either purchased ready-made in the typical diamond pattern or custom-made in a square or rectangular pattern, as well as various fan or ladder designs. Painting the wood changes the effect considerably. For example, white-painted lattice placed against a dark green house sets off a climbing 'New Dawn' rose perfectly.

Adding an overhead structure to a tall trellis, whether only a rafter and a few crossbars or a more elaborate construction that connects two trellises, brings a sense of enclosure. It also gives vines more space to expand and allows you to view the vines from below as well as from the side of the trellis. The step-by-step photos on pages 56–57 demonstrate how to plant vines to grow on a trellis.

A collection of climbing roses displayed on an open trellis includes the red-flowered 'Tempo' and the pink-flowered 'Cadenza'.

Vines in Containers

Vines with flexible trailing stems are ideal for planting in hanging baskets or planters and window boxes, bringing the vines' foliage and flowers to eye level. Use wire hanging baskets lined with moss or solid hanging planters made of wood or clay to decorate porches, patios, and decks. A series of hanging planters filled with cascading vines and fastened to an overhead structure around the perimeter of a deck or patio can provide a lot of privacy plus a shady retreat.

Window boxes, too, can benefit from the softening effect of small vines trailing over their edges and down the sides of the house. Boxes of this sort are also effective mounted on a plain fence, perhaps in a narrow side yard, where there is little ground space for planting.

A number of vines are suited to life in a large container or tub, where they can be supported by a small trellis or stakes or trained up a nearby post. Use pots to define the edges of decks and patios or as a feature near the front door. On a larger scale, a big planter box can serve as a very effective space divider or privacy screen on a patio. Build the box using 2 × 12 boards, 2 feet wide and as long as needed, and fit it with a trellis for vines.

Some clematis vines that grow well in containers with a support include the hybrid clematis 'Betty Corning', *C. texensis*, and *C. macropetala*. Miniature climbing roses, such as 'Hi-Ho', which grows 6 to 7 feet tall and has light red flowers, and 'Little Girl', only 4 to 5 feet tall with pink flowers, are beautiful

Sweet-potato vine (Ipomoea batatas), *asarina, and petunias cascade down the sides of a large container, creating a focal point on a terrace.*

A variegated form of English ivy (Hedera helix) *drapes the sides of a planter filled with caladiums and an ornamental grass* (Pennisetum *spp.*).

growing on small trellises in a container. Many annual vines are good choices, too, such as cardinal climber (Ipomoea × multifida), with its oddly cut leaves and clusters of bright red flowers, and Asarina scandens, a vigorous vine with soft green foliage and trumpet-shaped flowers of violet-blue, bright pink, or white. Sweet peas (Lathyrus odoratus) are wonderful in containers placed where their fragrance can be appreciated.

Combine vines in tubs with perennials, annuals, and small-scale ground covers like creeping speedwell (Veronica repens) to make a container creation that lasts all season.

Planting vines in movable containers is also a good way to grow some of the frost-tender climbers; you can move the whole pot to a protected spot in a garage, to a greenhouse, or indoors during winter. The fragrant true jasmines (Jasminum grandiflorum and J. officinale) and star jasmine (Trachelospermum jasminoides) can be grown this way, as well as the tender evergreen Mandevilla × amabilis 'Alice du Pont', which has beautiful 2- to 4-inch-wide pink flowers with yellow throats. The attractive foliage plant kangaroo vine (Cissus antarctica) also works well as a container plant taken outdoors in summer and moved back indoors in winter.

For instructions on how to plant vines in containers, see the text and step-by-step photos appearing on pages 62–63.

Vines for Hanging Baskets or Planters

Several smaller-growing vines provide foliage and flowers to furnish hanging planters. Sprenger asparagus (Asparagus densiflorus 'Sprengeri') has drooping stems 3 to 6 feet long clothed with bright green needlelike leaves. Bring it indoors for winter in cold climates.

Some miniature climbing roses, such as the bright Rosa 'Red Cascade', are good choices for hanging baskets. English ivy (Hedera helix), especially a small-leaved cultivar like 'Hahn's Self-Branching', also works well and looks good combined with other vines. A less vigorous variety of porcelain berry, Ampelopsis brevipedunculata 'Elegans', has leaves beautifully variegated with white and pink and makes an excellent hanging-basket plant. And for a quick and colorful summer accent, plant annual vines such as trailing nasturtiums (Tropaeolum majus) or morning-glories (Ipomoea tricolor) in hanging baskets.

Mandevilla × amabilis *blooms profusely in baskets as well as on trellises in a sheltered location.*

A variegated form of English ivy trails from a hanging basket containing a caladium, flowering begonias, and impatiens.

Vines That Ramble

Many vines grow as well along the ground as they do supported by a wall or trellis. Such vines become vigorous ground covers, rambling over large open areas or rough banks and suppressing weeds as they go. Some are also very effective at preventing erosion on slopes. Virginia creeper *(Parthenocissus quinquefolia)*, English ivy *(Hedera helix)*, and the memorial rose *(Rosa wichuraiana)* are examples of vines that form roots along their stems. As these roots grow into the soil, they stabilize the slope. You can encourage this rooting by pinning the stems to the ground with wire hooks or by piling a small mound of soil over the stems at intervals of a foot or two.

Be aware that these rooting vines and some others that ramble and spread—especially five-leaf akebia *(A. quinta)*, moonseed *(Menispermum canadense)*, Hall's honeysuckle *(Lonicera japonica* 'Halliana'*)*, trumpet creeper *(Campsis radicans)*, and the bittersweets *(Celastrus* spp.*)*—may become overly vigorous in situations where they are well adapted. They may then be difficult to control, spreading beyond the area you intended to cover into nearby trees and shrubs.

Ground-covering vines that are less invasive and more suitable for smaller areas include silver vein creeper *(Parthenocissus henryana)*, star jasmine *(Trachelospermum jasminoides)*, and wire vine *(Muehlenbeckia complexa)*, which forms a mat of dark-colored stems clothed with small, variably shaped leaves covering a bank or rock pile. In mild-winter climates, Cape honeysuckle *(Tecomaria capensis)* scrambles over banks, providing fine-textured foliage plus orange or scarlet flowers.

Silver lace vine (Polygonum aubertii) *can serve as a fast-growing screen for fences or buildings or as a rambling ground cover.*

Rambling Vines

The memorial rose (Rosa wichuraiana) *is a semievergreen rose that sprawls along the ground. Its dark green disease-resistant foliage sets off fragrant white flowers that bloom from late spring to fall. It makes a useful cover for large, rough banks.*

Perennial pea (Lathyrus latifolius), *a herbaceous flowering vine, has pretty blue-green foliage and, most commonly, reddish purple flowers; white- and pink-flowered forms are also available.*

Wintercreeper (Euonymus fortunei) *will grow as a ground cover or as a climber. Some especially good forms for ground-cover plantings include purple-leaved wintercreeper* (E. f. 'Colorata'), *whose leaves turn dark purple in fall and winter, and the variegated form* 'Gracilis', *which is more restrained in habit. A smaller species is* 'Kewensis', *whose leaves are only ¼ inch long; use it as dense, fine-textured ground cover for small areas.*

Algerian ivy (Hedera canariensis) *clothes a large slope with lush greenery, framing a patio and pool.*

Design Qualities of Vines

Climbing vines, whether supported by fences, arbors, or walls, or clambering by themselves up a tall tree, are usually planted to add a vertical dimension to the garden. However, many vines, especially those that cling to a support, also have an interesting horizontal aspect. The leaves of Boston ivy *(Partheno-cissus tricuspidata)*, for example, hang down in neatly layered horizontal rows; English ivy *(Hedera helix)* also gives this effect when grown on a building or fence. A tier of Dutchman's-pipe *(Aristolochia durior)*, wisteria *(Wisteria* spp.), or grapes *(Vitis* spp.*)* growing around a porch or on top of a pergola adds another sort of horizontal line to the garden.

Color from both foliage and flowers is, of course, a vital consideration when choosing vines. And just as with ground covers, foliage color, which lasts much longer than flower color, is a primary consideration. Besides shades of green that range from the mid-green of wisteria and most honeysuckles *(Lonicera* spp.*)* to the very dark green of some forms of English ivy to the blue-green of sweet pea *(Lathyrus odoratus)*, there are vines with golden and variegated foliage. The golden form of common hops *(Humulus lupulus* 'Aurea'*)* has large lime-yellow leaves that lighten the effect of darker shrubs or trees. 'Buttercup' is a cultivar of English ivy with yellow-green leaves.

English ivy also contributes cultivars with variegated leaves. 'Goldheart' has a bright splash of yellow on each leaf, while 'Glacier' has a cooling silvery gray and cream variegation. There is a handsome variegated form of star jasmine *(Trachelospermum jasminoides* 'Variegatum'*)* that has green foliage edged in cream. *Kolomikta actinidia,* silver vein creeper, and variegated euonymus have already been described.

The fall foliage color of some vines is a spectacular feature in the landscape, especially Virginia creeper *(Parthenocissus quinquefolia)*, Boston ivy, and the crimson glory vine *(Vitis coignetiae)*.

The foliage texture of vines is one of their most interesting qualities, especially as we can often see the leaves at eye level growing on a screen or trellis or draped over an arbor. The divided foliage of wisteria gives a lacy effect, even though the vine itself becomes very large and imposing. Jasmines have finely textured foliage that is effective for most of the year. Heavier textured foliage is evident in grape vines, kiwis *(Actinidia* spp.*)*, evergreen clematis *(C. armandii)*, and passionflower *(Passiflora* spp.*)*.

A gallery of colorful vines, clockwise from top left: Dr. Ruppell clematis, trumpet honeysuckle (Lonicera sempervirens), *bleeding-heart vine* (Clerodendrum thomsoniae), *and hyacinth bean* (Dolichos lablab).

Variegated Goldheart English ivy shows up well against a tree trunk.

The handsome divided leaves of Virginia creeper (Parthenocissus quinquefolia) *make interesting patterns against a stone wall.*

Growing up a tree trunk, the chartreuse leaves of Buttercup English ivy glow in the shade.

Golden clematis (C. tangutica) *displays its silvery seed heads throughout fall.*

Although many vines produce flowers, some of the showiest are those of the large-flowered hybrid clematis. Cultivars are available that bloom in spring, summer, and fall. Some favorites include white 'Henryi', pink 'Comtesse de Bouchard', blue-violet 'Ramona', and bicolored 'Nelly Moser'. At least a hundred other hybrids are available from specialty nurseries.

Climbing roses provide another immense selection of flower color. Besides such climbers as memorial rose *(Rosa wichuraiana)* and the rather tender evergreen Lady Banks rose *(R. banksiae)* with small white or yellow flowers, there are hundreds of old roses and hybrids available in all of the colors associated with shrub and hybrid tea roses.

Combining different vines with each other and with shrubs, trees, and ground covers brings out these elements of color and texture and often results in a longer season of interest in the garden. Planting Boston ivy with the variegated evergreen English ivy 'Glacier' on a wall provides year-round interest—and in fall the crimson leaves of the Boston ivy glow against the silver gray and cream of the English ivy. Or try planting a vine around a tree. Purple-leaved plum trees (among many other trees) can do double duty in the garden, blooming themselves in early spring and also supporting climbing roses with pink flowers, such as *Rosa* 'Dorothy Perkins' or 'Cecile Brunner'.

CHAPTER 2

Planting Lawns, Ground Covers & Vines

gardeners know that planting can be hard work. But it is also satisfying and has definite rewards. • Paying attention at the outset to details of soil preparation, fertilizing, and watering will give you healthier lawns, ground covers, or vines that look the way you want them to. • This chapter will show you how to perform these tasks efficiently and effectively, so that you can enjoy your garden more immediately and spend less time on maintenance in the future.

Starting a Lawn

*T*he best time of year to plant a lawn depends on your climate and the planting method you use. Cool-season grasses are planted either from seed or sod. Seed is less expensive, but it takes more work to get the lawn established. A wider variety of grass species is available from seed, however, enabling you to choose the grass or mixture of grasses that will grow best in your lawn. Sod is easier to care for after installation and looks good almost instantly.

Early fall is the best time to start cool-season grasses from seed. The soil is still warm, but air temperatures are not as hot as in midsummer. You can also sow seed in early spring, but it takes a long time for the grass to germinate and become established in the cool soil, giving weeds time to outgrow the lawn. Sod of cool-season grasses can be installed any time the soil isn't frozen, although it's advisable to avoid very hot weather that will stress the grass and necessitate extra irrigation.

Although common Bermuda grass can be planted from seed, many of the warm-season grasses are planted from sprigs, stolons, plugs, or sod, as they don't set viable seed. Sprigs and the similar stolons are 3- to 6-inch-long pieces of grass stem; they should have some roots or at least intact joints from which roots can grow. Plugs are small pieces cut from sod, 2 to 4 inches across. Spring is the best time to plant either plant parts or seeds, as the warming weather provides ideal growing conditions for these grasses.

Before planting your lawn, it is a good idea to test your soil to see what it needs for plants to grow well. It may, for example, benefit from extra organic matter, certain fertilizers, or amendments to alter the pH level (see the sidebar on page 48 for more on pH).

The soft velvet green of a new lawn complements a densely planted garden of trees, shrubs, and ground covers.

1 Before laying sod, dig in organic material and fertilizer, rake, and then firm soil with a roller so that it is an inch below surrounding surfaces.

2 Use a wheelbarrow to move the heavy rolls of turf to the new lawn area, a few at a time. Keep the rolls lightly moistened.

3 Unroll the sod against a straight edge, one strip at a time. Handle the strips of sod gently to avoid tearing or stretching them.

4 One way to lay the strips is in a brick-bond pattern. Firm the edges with your fingers, after making sure the sod fits tightly together.

5 Lay additional turf to close any gaps. Use a heavy knife to cut the sod to fit around trees, sprinkler heads, and the final edges of the lawn.

6 Fill in small gaps in the seams with good soil. Use a water-filled roller to ensure good contact between sod and soil. Water thoroughly.

Starting a Lawn CONTINUED

Soil pH

Soil pH, a measure of how acid or alkaline the soil is, affects the solubility of various minerals in the soil that are necessary to plant growth. If plants can't take up the dissolved minerals through their roots, they won't grow properly. Most plants (including lawn grasses) do best within a range of 5.5 to 7.5; a pH of 6.5 is optimum. Add ground limestone to raise the pH of very acid soil (below 6). A pH over 7.5 (indicating alkaline soil) can be lowered by adding elemental sulfur. A soil test will indicate whether either of these amendments is needed and in what quantity.

1 To seed a lawn, remove any existing turf, then till the area. Rake out debris and dig in organic material.

2 Go over the area several times with a rake to level the soil. Be sure to fill low areas and smooth out high areas.

5 On a windless day, sow the seeds as evenly as possible. Rake them lightly into the soil, burying them ⅛ inch deep.

6 Cover the seedbed with a floating row cover to protect the seeds from birds. Use a sprinkler to water thoroughly.

3 Add lime to the soil, if needed, to adjust the pH. Spread a fertilizer recommended for new lawns over the area.

4 Rake again, and roll to firm the soil. If the soil is dry, water a day or so before seeding.

7 Water often until seeds germinate, between 14 and 21 days. Remove the row cover when grass begins to grow.

8 As the grass grows, decrease the frequency of irrigation, but increase the amount of water applied each time.

Starting a Lawn CONTINUED

TROUBLESHOOTING TIP

Plant warm-season grasses, such as hybrid Bermuda, St. Augustine, and zoysia, by using sprigs, stolons, or plugs or by sodding. Planting living pieces of grass is the only way to establish these grasses, as they don't set viable seed. Buy sprigs or plugs from mail-order firms or from a sod farm, following their advice on the quantity to order. When the plants arrive, be sure to store them in a shady spot and keep them moist, and plant as soon as possible.

With this information you can avoid adding unnecessary amendments, which may percolate through the soil and contaminate lakes or groundwater. You can buy soil test kits at most nurseries or have a professional laboratory perform the test; check with your county cooperative extension agent for information on laboratories.

Before digging or tilling, remove any existing lawn, using a power sod cutter or a sharp spade; also get rid of any debris, such as rocks and lumber. You can eliminate existing weeds by hoeing. As there will be weed seeds in the soil, water the area and wait a few days for them to germinate and then hoe again. If time allows, repeat this cycle one or two more times. You may wish to use a glyphosate-based herbicide that kills most weeds. It breaks down on contact with the soil, so you can plant a week after treatment. (Follow all directions, taking care not to spray plants you want to keep.)

Next, establish a rough grade, using a heavy rake to smooth high spots and fill low ones. Install mowing strips (see page 12), if desired. Spread 3 or 4 inches of organic material, such as compost, nitrogen-fortified ground bark or sawdust, rotted manure, or peat moss, over the soil. Organic material makes clay soil looser and easier to work and helps it drain better; in sandy soil, it holds nutrients and water. Also add fertilizer as recommended by your soil test. If you didn't do a soil test, try a 7-21-7 fertilizer, which contains a high percentage of phosphorous (as indicated by the middle number), a nutrient that is especially important in establishing lawn grasses.

Dig all of these materials into the top 6 to 8 inches of soil with a shovel, or make several passes over the area with a rotary tiller. Rake again to smooth the soil, then go over the area with a roller (half-filled with water to give it weight) to firm the soil, making a good base for sod or seeds. For additional instructions on laying sod, refer to the step-by-step photos on page 47; for sowing seed, see the photos on pages 48–49.

▼ Planting Sprigs or Stolons

There are several methods for planting sprigs or stolons of warm-season grasses. The fastest is to broadcast shredded stems (specify that you want to use this method when ordering) over the area just like seeds, covering lightly with soil; this can be somewhat wasteful, as some of the sprigs will be buried too deeply to grow. Another way is to use a hoe to dig 3-inch-deep furrows in the soil from 4 to 12 inches apart (the closer spacing will fill in faster) and plant the sprigs so that the foliage is above ground level. A third method is to place the sprigs in a grid pattern, 6 inches apart each way, and press each into the soil with a notched stick. Whichever method you choose, roll the area with a roller half-filled with water to firm the soil around the sprigs. Water at once and then daily until the sprigs start growing.

The lawn area will look patchy at first, but as the sprigs grow and spread horizontally, they will fill in to make a solid carpet. Mowing, beginning when the young plants are about 3 inches tall, helps the grass spread. Be sure to use a mower with a sharp blade to avoid tearing the delicate young grasses or pulling them out of the soil.

As warm-season grasses naturally turn brown in winter, many homeowners in mild-winter climates overseed their lawn in mid-fall with annual or perennial rye. These grasses stay green all winter but do require some irrigation and mowing.

Perennial ryegrass is a popular cool-season grass, planted from seed or sod.

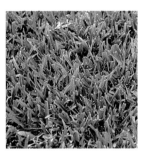

Zoysia, started from sod, sprigs, or plugs, is a drought-tolerant warm-season grass.

1 Many warm-season grasses are planted from plugs, sold in trays. Keep the tray moist and shaded until you plant.

2 Prepare the soil as for sod or seed lawns. Plant the plugs 6 inches apart in a grid pattern.

3 To distribute your weight evenly, stand on a board. After planting, roll the area to firm the soil around the plugs; water well.

4 The lawn looks patchy at first but soon fills in with regular watering. Mowing once the grass reaches 3 inches helps it spread.

Planting Ground Covers

*T*he best time to plant ground covers in mild-winter regions is fall, giving the roots time to grow and become established during the cool part of the year. In cold-winter areas, plant in early spring, as soon as the soil can be worked, to give the plants a long growing season before freezing weather arrives.

Careful soil preparation will help ensure that your ground covers get off to a fast start, covering the ground and suppressing weed growth as quickly as possible. Have your soil tested and follow the advice of the laboratory to alter the pH, if necessary, or choose a ground cover adapted to your soil.

Remove sod or weeds, just as for lawn (see page 50). For most ground covers, also spread organic matter and fertilizer (use a balanced 10-10-10 fertilizer applied at the rate recommended on the bag) over the whole area. Dig or till these amendments into the soil, then rake to level. However, if you are planting woody ground-cover shrubs like junipers, ceanothus, or bearberry (*Arctostaphylos* spp.), you don't need to dig up the entire area; remove weeds, then add fertilizer to each planting hole.

If you are planting a ground cover under a shade tree or large shrub, the roots of the tree or shrub will compete with the ground cover for nutrients and water. Again, spread a generous layer of organic matter and till it into the soil; this inevitably severs some surface roots but seldom seriously harms a mature tree or shrub. Avoid piling new soil over the roots, or they may suffocate. Sometimes the roots are too thick and too close to the surface to allow digging or tilling. In this case it's better to simply spread an attractive mulch, as ground covers are unlikely to grow well.

Ground covers are sold in small containers, cell packs containing four or six plants, or larger 1- or 2-gallon pots, or you can buy them as rooted cuttings in flats. Whichever size you buy, look for young, healthy plants, checking to see that the roots are not circling inside the container or growing out of the drainage holes, indicating a pot-bound plant.

How far apart to space the plants depends on the particular ground cover, how fast you want it to fill in, and your budget—that is, how many plants you can afford to buy. Most ground covers can be spaced 6 to 12 inches apart (see the encyclopedia beginning on page 100 for general guidelines on spacing). The closer spacing will give you fast coverage. Wider spacing requires fewer plants, but you will need to weed for an extra season before the ground cover grows together.

Set small plants in holes just deep enough for the root ball and slightly wider. For larger plants, dig a hole that tapers outward at the bottom, leaving a platform of firm soil in the middle on which to set the root ball. Loosen the roots and place the plant in the hole, firming soil around it.

Water the plants well immediately after planting. Continue to water every few days for the first few weeks if there is no rain. Adding a 2-inch layer of mulch of pine needles or straw around the plants helps maintain even soil moisture and slows weed growth, enabling your ground cover to establish itself more quickly. Be careful not to place mulch on the crowns of the plants, which could cause rot. And pull any weeds that do appear.

1 *To plant on a slope, clean out the area, pulling weeds and other unwanted plants.*

2 *Be sure to completely remove roots of perennial weeds, or they may resprout.*

3 *If the slope is fairly steep, install a retainer to hold the soil in place.*

4 *Incorporate several inches of compost or other organic material. Rake the surface smooth.*

5 *Set out plants in a staggered pattern, so that they will eventually fill in the area completely.*

6 *Cover the slope with wire netting to hold the soil in place until the roots begin to grow.*

Planting a Wildflower Meadow or Prairie

*E*stablishing a meadow or prairie containing a mixture of flowering annuals, perennials, and bunchgrasses is similar to planting a lawn or ground cover. Clearing the area of existing sod or weeds is essential. Native wildflowers and grasses are tough plants once established, but while still young they can't compete with sod-forming grasses or weeds.

Use a power sod cutter or sharp spade to get rid of the lawn. Water, then wait for remaining pieces of lawn and weeds to grow and dig them out. You can also use a glyphosphate-based herbicide to kill sod or weeds. Rake up or till in the dead vegetation. Other alternatives are soil solarization and smothering the sod and weeds with black plastic or boards, which cut off sunlight. Leave the covering in place for at least two or three months during the growing season. Rake the soil smooth before planting.

In the South and West, plant in fall to take advantage of seasonal rains and cool weather. In colder regions, early spring is best for planting.

To plant a meadow or prairie, use plants, seeds, or a combination of both. Setting out year-old plants that you buy or start in advance gives faster results than seeding. Most will bloom the first year they are installed. Set plants approximately a foot apart, but somewhat randomly, spacing some more closely and some farther apart. Plant in drifts or masses of one species and interweave at the edges with other species to help give a natural effect.

To sow seeds, first mix one part seeds with four parts potting soil or sand to help distribute the seeds evenly. You can either broadcast seeds of mixed species evenly over the whole area or scatter each individual species' seeds in its own area, with some overlap to blend into neighboring areas.

After sowing, rake lightly to cover the seeds. Water if it doesn't rain, and continue to water for the first two months after planting whenever the soil becomes dry. Keep the meadow weeded until the plants are well established and blooming. Be patient! It will take two or three years before the plants begin to bloom.

A mowed path leads through a meadow of wildflowers, including Culver's root (Veronicastrum virginicum), *compass plant* (Silphium laciniatum), *and beebalm* (Monarda didyma).

Planting Vines

Starting vines from seed is an inexpensive way to quickly cover a fence or trellis or to experiment with unusual vines. Vines to grow from seed include annuals and a number of fast-growing frost-tender vines that are perennial in mild-winter climates but are treated like annuals in cold climates. Seeds of many interesting hardy vines are available, too.

Annual vines (or perennials grown as annuals) that need a fairly long season—three or four months—before blooming are best started indoors in March or April. These include cup-and-saucer vine *(Cobaea scandens)*, black-eyed Susan vine *(Thunbergia alata)*, and the exotic Chilean glory vine *(Eccremocarpus scaber)*. Seeds of some vines, such as canary creeper *(Tropaeolum peregrinum)*, morning-glory *(Ipomoea tricolor)*, and sweet pea *(Lathyrus odoratus)*, can either be sown indoors (in cold climates) or outdoors

in their permanent location. A few annual vines grow better if directly seeded outdoors, as their roots are easily damaged in transplanting; this category includes gourds *(Cucurbita pepo* var. *ovifera* and *Lagenaria siceraria)*, scarlet runner beans *(Phaseolus coccineus)*, and nasturtiums *(Tropaeolum majus)*.

To start seeds indoors, fill clean flats of 4-inch pots to within 1 inch of the top with dampened commercial potting mix. Check the seed packet for the exact sowing depth. Gently press the mix down over the seeds. Now, water; to avoid washing the seeds out of the mix, place the pots in a pan with a few inches of water for an hour or so. Then let the pots drain, and place in a warm spot indoors until the seeds germinate. Keep the soil mix evenly moist.

When the seedlings have grown two sets of true leaves (which have the same characteristics as those of

1 *After unpacking, soak the roots of a bare-root vine before planting. Dig a hole the depth of the roots, leaving a cone of soil in the middle.*

2 *Spread the roots over the cone of soil. Fill around the roots with soil, and firm in place with your hands. Water the plant thoroughly.*

Planting Vines CONTINUED

the mature plant), thin or transplant them. Cut off extra plants with small scissors, or carefully separate them and transplant into individual 4-inch pots. Water thoroughly and place on a sunny windowsill or under fluorescent lights set 6 inches above the tops of the seedlings. Give each a small wooden or bamboo stake to grow on—that way you won't have to untangle the vines later and risk breaking them. Use a half-strength liquid fertilizer every week.

Wait until the danger of frost is over to transplant the vines into the garden. A week before, acclimate the seedlings to outdoor conditions by placing them outside in a sheltered spot or in a cold frame protected from frost. Transplant the young vines into well-prepared soil next to their permanent support. Use the temporary stakes to help lead the vines in the manner you want them to grow.

If you don't use seeds, buy vines as bare-root plants or in 1-gallon or larger containers. Container-grown vines are available in spring, summer, and fall. Bare-root vines, such as grapes, climbing roses, and clematis, are generally sold in late winter.

You can plant hardy vines in either fall or spring. It is best, however, to wait until spring to set out vines that may be slightly frost tender in your climate to give them plenty of time to become established. In cooler climates, if the heat is not intense, vines can be planted in summer, but they will need more frequent watering.

When shopping for vines at a local nursery or garden center, choose plants that look healthy and don't have constricted roots. Check that the roots are not circling inside the container or growing out of the drainage holes, indicating a pot-bound plant. Look especially carefully for signs of pests or diseases, examining growing tips, undersides of leaves, and leaf

1 *Before planting a vine on a trellis, fasten the trellis securely to the wall. Most vines eventually become quite heavy.*

5 *Gently thread the stems of the vine up and through the bars of the trellis.*

2 *Dig the planting hole, adding compost as you work. Remove the root ball from the pot, cutting it if necessary.*

3 *Remove the short trellis used to support the vine in the container. You can also wait to remove it until after planting.*

4 *Center the plant in the hole. Firm the soil around it to ensure good contact between the root and soil.*

6 *Fasten the stems loosely to the trellis with twist ties or flexible plastic tape.*

7 *Water well to settle the roots in place and eliminate any air pockets.*

8 *Spread a few inches of mulch, such as shredded leaves, around the plant.*

Planting Vines CONTINUED

1 *To pregerminate morning-glory seeds, roll them between several layers of damp paper towels and store in a plastic bag until roots emerge (about a week).*

2 *Carefully plant the seeds about 1 inch deep in loosened soil near netting or a fence you'd like to cover. Set them 6 to 8 inches apart. Water well.*

3 *As they grow, lead the young vines toward the nearby netting or fence. The plants will soon climb upward.*

4 *By midsummer the morning-glories will decorate the fence with their colorful flowers.*

1 When planting near a tree, fasten chicken wire loosely around the trunk base to help the vine start climbing.

2 Dig a planting hole. Remove the plant from the container, cutting the pot, if necessary.

3 Center the plant in the hole. Firm soil around the root ball. Water well and spread mulch.

4 Guide the stems of the vine through the chicken wire, spreading them around the tree trunk.

TROUBLESHOOTING TIP

Planting a vine to grow through or around a host tree or shrub can give beautiful results. The host plant should already be well established and strong enough to carry the weight of the vine. Also consider how the vine climbs. Avoid vigorous twiners that can strangle the host tree.

Dig the climber's planting hole outside the root spread of the host, and use a stake to lead the vine to the tree or shrub. Use wire ties or mesh around the trunk or stems of a host plant to help the vine climb. Check occasionally to be sure they are not strangling the host.

Planting Vines CONTINUED

Planting Clematis

Clematis, especially the large-flowered hybrid types, grow best if planted where their roots will remain cool—for example, on the north or east side of a hedge, trellis, or host plant, such as a large shrub. They require a soil that is fertile and holds moisture.

Plant clematis so that the crown (where stem meets roots) will be covered by 2 inches of soil. This allows new basal buds to develop underground. Protect the brittle young stems from damage with a temporary collar of wire netting. Finally, spread a thick mulch around the vines and do not let them dry out.

axils (where leaf meets stem). Finally, keep in mind that vines with branching stems, rather than one central stem, are easier to train on a trellis or wall.

Near house walls and fences, where you often want to plant vines, the soil may be compacted and of poor quality. If so, dig a hole 1½ to 2 feet wide and deep. Mix some of the excavated topsoil with compost, well-aged manure, or damp peat moss, plus ½ cup of an all-purpose fertilizer (such as 10-10-10). Refill the hole halfway. If the soil is already reasonably fertile and easy to work, you won't need to dig such a large hole. Simply fork in a 2-inch layer of compost and a sprinkle of fertilizer, then dig a hole that tapers outward at the bottom, with a platform of firm soil in the middle on which to set the root ball. Set up trellises, tripods, or other supports for your vines before you actually plant them to avoid damaging roots and stems later on.

Make sure the roots are moist before planting. If the stem of a container-grown vine is tied to a stake, leave it in place for now. Center the vine in the planting hole at about a 45-degree angle leaning toward its support. Spread out the roots, and check that the top of the roots or root ball will be level with the surrounding soil. (Clematis, however, is planted more deeply; see the sidebar above.) Fill the hole, firming soil around the roots, and water the vine well.

If the vine is attached to a stake or small trellis in the pot, gently untie it before or after planting. Spread out the stems, cutting out any damaged or very weak ones. If the stems aren't long enough yet to reach their support, insert a temporary stake behind each one, leading to the support, and tie the stem loosely to it with plastic nursery tape.

Plant woodbine honeysuckle (Lonicera periclymenum *var.* serotina 'Florida') *near a path where its fragrant and colorful blossoms can best be appreciated.*

Cover the soil with a 2-inch layer of mulch, such as bark chips or shredded leaves. Keep newly planted vines moist, but not soggy, and check frequently to see that the stems are growing in the direction you want, tying them to the support when necessary.

Here is a good location for clematis: The roots are shaded by a ground cover, while the leaves and flowers receive more sunlight. This cultivar is 'The President'.

Planting Vines in Containers

EARTH·WISE TIP

Superabsorbent polymers are added to potting mixes or garden soil to help retain water. The polymers absorb hundreds of times their weight in water and give plants a source of moisture even after the soil itself dries out. This means you water less often. The polymers also hold dissolved nutrients, so fertilizers needn't be replenished as frequently.

Polymer products are available at many nurseries. Mix the polymers with water and add them to your potting mix in the proportion recommended by the manufacturer.

Many vines grow well in containers. Northern gardeners can grow tender tropical vines by using containers and moving them indoors for winter. Pots and tubs help control vigorous vines that spread too invasively to be cultivated directly in a small garden. Some vines, especially nonwoody annuals and tender perennials such as black-eyed Susan vine *(Thunbergia alata)*, nasturtiums *(Tropaeolum majus)*, and morning-glories *(Ipomoea tricolor)*, can be planted in hanging baskets, with their long stems trailing.

For a hardy perennial vine, choose a container that is large enough to accommodate the vine for at least a year. If you are planting from a 1-gallon nursery pot, use a container 10 or 12 inches wide and at least 10 inches deep; use a larger container if you plan to surround the vine with other plants. Be sure the pot has

a drainage hole and is frost-proof if it will be outdoors in cold winters.

Use a porous, open-textured potting soil, which will hold moisture for the roots yet drain freely. The soil mix should allow roots to penetrate easily. A mix of equal parts good garden soil and compost, plus some sharp builder's sand, perlite, or vermiculite, is suitable for large tubs that remain outdoors all year. Or, add one part sharp sand to two parts of a packaged potting mix plus an all-purpose packaged organic fertilizer. Garden soil alone stays too soggy and forms a dense mass that roots have difficulty growing in.

Before planting, cover the drainage hole with a curved pot shard or a piece of fine-mesh screen to prevent the soil mix from falling out. Set a trellis or stakes, if needed, in the pot near the edge, and partially fill the pot with damp potting mix to stabilize the trellis and make a base for the root ball.

Moisten the soil in the nursery container before transplanting to your larger pot. To remove the vine from the nursery container, turn the pot upside down and tap its rim against a solid object, using your other hand to support the root ball as it slides out. If the roots are compacted, loosen them with your fingers to let them grow out into the new soil.

Set the vine in the new container on top of the base of potting mix, and check that the top of the root ball is 1 or 2 inches below the rim. Fill around the roots with potting soil, tapping it in the container with a stick or your hands as you work. Tie the stems of the vine to their trellis or stakes (or a nearby post) to help them begin their ascent.

Water well to settle the potting mix around the vine, adding more mix if it settles too much. Check daily to see that the plants are moist. The general rule is to water as soon as the top inch of soil feels dry.

1 *Insert small plants of a trailing ground cover or vine, such as* Vinca major *'Variegata', around the edges of a balcony planter. They will drape gracefully over the sides.*

1 To plant a wire hanging basket, set the basket on an outdoor table. Use a clay pot to steady the basket.

2 Line the basket with a circle of moist sheet moss, and fill with a light packaged potting mix.

3 Place the plants (nasturtiums are shown here) in the center and around the edges of the basket.

4 Water well and let drain. Hang the basket with attached chains. Water frequently, as it will dry out quickly.

Creating Mulched Areas

A mulched area of the garden can be a good-looking, relatively inexpensive, and low-maintenance alternative to lawn or ground covers in areas where poor soil, shallow tree roots, or dense shade makes plants difficult to maintain. Mulch doesn't last as long as hard surfaces like brick or concrete patios, but it is much easier and less expensive to install. And mulches, unlike concrete or asphalt, allow water to penetrate into the soil without wasteful runoff.

Wood products such as shredded bark and ground bark chips are often used for mulched areas. Ground bark, made from fir, pine, hemlock, or redwood, is available in ¼-inch to 2½-inch chips. Although all these mulches can take foot traffic, the smaller chips are more comfortable to walk on. Consider including stepping stones or installing a hard-surfaced path across a mulched area that gets a lot of traffic.

To discourage weed growth and look good, a bark or chip mulch should be at least 3 inches deep. To keep costs down on a large mulched area, use tree chips (often free from tree maintenance firms and municipalities) for the bottom inch or so. Put landscape fabric (see tip on page 52) under the mulch to further reduce weed problems. Don't lay solid sheets of black plastic under mulch because the plastic restricts movement of water and air into the soil; in time the sheets also tear and show through the thin spots in the mulch.

Install an edging or header to help keep the mulch chips in place. Grade the soil, and set the edging with its top 3 inches above grade. Headers made of redwood, landscape timbers, or railroad ties blend well with mulches made of wood products.

Spread wood chips at least 3 inches deep to discourage weed growth. Smaller chips are best for a path, as they are easier to walk on.

Gravel looks good as a mulch or on a path in a garden of drought-resistant plants.

Buying Mulches

Look for sources of wood-product mulches and gravel in the Yellow Pages under Building Materials, Landscape Equipment and Supplies, Rock, or Stone.

Wood mulches are sold in bags or in bulk. A 2-cubic-foot bag will cover an area of 8 square feet about 3 inches deep. When buying in bulk, estimate that 1 cubic yard will cover 108 square feet, also 3 inches deep. How much gravel to order varies somewhat with the size of the gravel, but generally a ton of rock covers 100 square feet.

Shredded bark and chips are organic materials, so they will break down and need replenishing after a year or two. If you ever plan to convert the mulched area to garden, sprinkle a high-nitrogen fertilizer over the decomposing wood before adding fresh mulch. Wood products take nitrogen from the soil as they break down.

Gravel or pebbles make more permanent mulches because they don't break down and are heavier and more difficult to remove. Stone is more expensive than wood products but not as costly as brick or concrete. Gravel comes in a wide range of textures, colors, and sizes that can harmonize with plants, large rocks, and other hard surfaces. Stone from local quarries may blend best with your surroundings and be less expensive than imported materials. When choosing gravel or pebbles, take home samples to check color and texture combinations in your yard.

Crushed rock gives firm footing on paths, but it has sharp edges. Smooth river rock, such as pea gravel, is easier to walk on. Larger river rock isn't meant for foot traffic, but it makes an attractive mulch around trees. If a tree is not reliably hardy in your area, a stone mulch will help by absorbing heat on sunny days and slowly radiating it back into the atmosphere at night.

For a long-lasting rock mulch, first grade the site and install an edging so that its top is 2 inches above grade. If you want, lay landscape fabric on top of the smoothed soil. Using a heavy-duty wheelbarrow, spread a base layer of decomposed granite or construction sand about an inch deep. With an iron rake, level the base, then moisten it. Use a heavy roller to compress and settle the base. Now spread at least 2 inches of gravel mulch, and roll again to compress the gravel into place. Gravel surfaces are easy to maintain, requiring only periodic raking to remove debris.

CHAPTER 3

Maintaining the Lawn

*t*he major aspects of lawn maintenance—mowing, watering, fertilizing, weeding, and pest control—are closely interrelated. How you manage each affects all of the others; together they determine the appearance of your lawn and how healthy it is. • With a little experimentation, it's not difficult to settle on a lawn-care routine that suits your schedule and the needs of your lawn. While these tasks may seem arduous at first, they can actually be quite enjoyable and rewarding. • You may, over time, come to look forward to contemplative time spent tending your lawn.

General Maintenance

Mowing Heights

Vertically growing grasses, such as Kentucky bluegrass, are cut taller to avoid removing too much of the leaf blade. Spreading sorts, like Bermuda grass, should be cut lower to help prevent thatch buildup. Here are recommended mower settings in inches for common grasses:

Bahia grass, 2–3

Bermuda grass, 1–1½

Hybrid Bermuda grass, ½–1

Buffalo grass, 1½–2

Fine fescue, 1½–2½

Kentucky bluegrass, 1½–2½

Perennial rye, 1½–2½

St. Augustine, 2–3

Tall fescue, 1½–3

Zoysia, 1–2

*P*erhaps more than any other type of gardening, lawn care requires solid gardening knowledge rather than a "green thumb." A few simple routines applied to this knowledge will result in a lush, beautiful expanse of grass.

▼ Mowing

In addition to helping your lawn look properly maintained, mowing affects its overall health and how much water and fertilizer it requires. How often you need to mow depends on the time of year and the type of grass you have. Cool-season grasses grow fastest and consequently need more frequent mowing in spring and fall, while warm-season grasses must be mowed more often in summer. Thus, an every-Saturday-no-matter-what mowing schedule from spring through fall doesn't necessarily match the actual growth pattern of your grass. It's better to watch your lawn and mow it when it needs mowing.

As a rule of thumb, lawns should be mowed when the grass is about a third taller than the height recommended for your species of grass (see the sidebar at left for mowing heights). For example, Kentucky bluegrass, which is healthiest at a height of about 2 inches, should be cut when it reaches 3 inches. If you let the lawn grow too tall and then cut off half or more of its growth, the grass plants will be weakened, as the lower leaves and stems that were shaded are suddenly exposed to the sun, causing the grass to turn yellow. This also shocks the root system, which may stop growing for a time. Research has shown that lawns kept fairly consistently at the correct height grow deeper roots and therefore need less frequent irrigation and are better able to withstand drought. They are also denser, with less open soil where weeds can grow.

Leaving grass clippings on the lawn to decompose can also lead to a healthier lawn. The clippings contain 3 to 6 percent nitrogen, ½ to 1 percent phosphorous, and 1 to 3 percent potassium as well as calcium and other nutrients. University experiments have shown that when clippings are removed, lawns require as much as 2 extra pounds of nitrogen each year, which you have to purchase and spread. Because clippings are green grass blades that break down readily, they don't contribute to thatch, which is a buildup of woody tissues. Frequent mowing (or the use of a mulching mower) produces short clippings that filter down to soil level and decompose quickly. If longer clippings form a mat on top of the grass, blocking sunlight and air, remove and compost them.

▼ Watering

Deciding when and how much to water your lawn depends on the type of grass you have, the kind of soil in your yard, and the weather. Like mowing, watering is best done when the lawn actually needs it rather than on a predetermined schedule.

Overwatering is wasteful and can invite disease. It also causes the grass to grow faster and need more frequent mowing. On the other hand, underwatering a lawn leads to a shallow root system that dries out too quickly in warm or windy weather. Try to apply enough water to moisten the entire root zone (the top 4 to 8 inches of soil). Note that grasses such as Bermuda grass, buffalo grass, tall fescue, St. Augustine, and zoysia naturally grow deeper roots (assuming the soil is moist) than such shallow-rooted species as Kentucky bluegrass and perennial rye. Watering below the reach of the roots is just as counterproductive as watering too shallowly.

To grow a healthy lawn, it is important to establish a regular program of mowing, watering, fertilizing, weeding, and pest control.

Whether you use hose-end sprinklers or install an underground irrigation system, be sure to overlap areas of coverage for a uniform application of water. Since clay soils absorb water more slowly, it may be necessary to irrigate for two or more short periods to avoid runoff and assure that the water penetrates deeply enough. Clay soil, however, holds water longer, so you won't need to water as frequently. Sandy soil absorbs water quickly and should be watered more frequently, applying less water each time, so that the moisture doesn't move below the root zone.

In very hot or windy weather your lawn uses more water. Shaded lawns need less water, unless the grass is competing with tree roots for moisture.

With all these variables, check occasionally to see how moist your soil actually is and how deep the moisture goes. To determine the moisture, dig a hole with a shovel, replacing the turf after examining it, or use a soil-sampling tube, which removes a core of soil. Pushing a long screwdriver into the soil is another method; it will move readily through moist, but not dry, soil.

Water the lawn when the top inch or two of soil is dry. The best time to water is in early morning, even before dawn, when there is both less evaporation and less wind.

▼ Fertilizing

It's not easy to make decisions about how, when, or with what product to fertilize your lawn. But it helps to consider which nutrients the grass may actually need and how they become available to the grass plants. Nitrogen is necessary for grass to grow and spread. Too much nitrogen, however, causes the grass to grow too quickly, requiring frequent mowing, and makes it susceptible to disease. Phosphorous aids in root growth and is especially vital in establishing grass from seed. A small amount is also necessary for healthy growth of mature lawns. A bit of potassium is important as well, helping to make lawn grasses tougher and more resistant to adverse conditions like drought, heat, and cold.

Fertilizers that supply these nutrients (and sometimes other micronutrients, such as calcium and sulfur), are classified as either synthetic (chemically

General Maintenance CONTINUED

Insect-Resistant Lawn Grasses

Certain varieties of perennial ryegrass, turf-type tall fescues, and fine fescues live in a symbiotic relationship with a group of naturally occurring beneficial fungi called endophytes. These fungi produce toxins that repel insects such as chinch bugs, sod webworms, billbugs, armyworms, and aphids. Endophytes can be introduced to the lawn only through seed, and the seed must be less than a year old to be effective. Check the seed label to learn the age of the seed and whether endophytes are present.

derived, as with ammonium nitrate) or organic (derived from the remains or a by-product of a once-living organism, as with blood meal or manure). Many chemical fertilizers contain a high proportion of fast-acting water-soluble nitrogen. Although this gives the grass a quick boost, much of it is carried below the root zone by rain or irrigation and may eventually pollute groundwater, lakes, and rivers.

Lawn-care experts are frequently recommending slow-release or nonsoluble fertilizers, which have ingredients that are converted by natural organisms in the soil into forms plants can use. These provide a steady diet for the lawn, keeping it growing well but not at an excessive speed. Slow-release fertilizers are available in both synthetic-based formulations and as natural organic blends.

A soil test, either from a soil laboratory or a home test kit, is the best way to decide how much of which nutrients your lawn really needs. Remember to check the soil's pH at the same time (see the sidebar on page 48). If you lack a soil test, and assuming that grass clippings are left on the lawn, start with 3 or 4 pounds of actual nitrogen per 1,000 square feet of lawn per year, plus about 1/2 pound of phosphorous, and a pound of potassium. Note that these recommendations are given in actual pounds of nitrogen (or phosphorous or potassium). To calculate the number of pounds of nitrogen in, for example, a 20-pound bag of 10-5-5 fertilizer, multiply 20 (the bag's total weight) by 10 percent (the percentage of nitrogen, as shown by the first number of the nitrogen-phosphorous-potassium ratio on the bag) to find that there are 2 pounds of actual nitrogen in the bag.

The best time of year to fertilize depends on the type of lawn you have. Cool-season lawns should receive about three-quarters of their total fertilizer in several applications in fall, when roots are building food reserves that will last them through the next summer. Spread the remaining amount of fertilizer in early spring. Feed warm-season lawns several times in spring and summer during their peak growth period.

You can broadcast fertilizer by hand—safest with organic or other slow-release fertilizers that are less likely to burn the grass if fertilizer is accidentally applied too thickly in one spot. Mechanical spreaders give more even coverage. There are hand-operated broadcasters, which are good for small lawns, and walk-behind broadcasters or drop-spreaders, which are more convenient for large lawns. Water the lawn after you have fertilized it.

▼ Weeding

Keeping your lawn properly mowed, watered, and fertilized so that it is growing steadily is the best defense against weeds. With little bare soil, weeds cannot easily germinate and grow. The next best defense is to inspect your lawn frequently and pull out any weeds that do appear before they become large and difficult to pull or, worse, go to seed. A weeding tool or a small trowel helps get all of the root out and prevents regrowth; this is especially important for removing dandelions and other weeds that have deep taproots.

Herbicides may seem like an easy alternative to weeding by hand, but they can be dangerous poisons. If used incorrectly they may damage or even kill your lawn or other plants, and they can contaminate the environment outside your garden. If you decide to use an herbicide, identify the weeds you are trying to kill (get help from your county cooperative extension agent or nursery personnel) to be sure you are using the correct herbicide. Follow the directions on the label exactly, noting how long after application children and pets must be kept off the lawn.

▼ Controlling Pests and Diseases

Dozens of different sorts of insects may live in or near your lawn without ever harming it. In fact, most are a normal and beneficial part of your garden's ecosystem. Thus, before you reach for harmful sprays, it is important to be certain any brown spots or other damage you notice on your lawn are actually caused by insects and not by dog urine, spilled fertilizer, or a dry area the sprinklers missed. Look closely at the grass to locate insects you think are harmful. As with weeds, if you can't identify an insect, take it to your county cooperative extension agent or a nursery.

There are a number of nonchemical treatments for lawn insects. Milky spore disease is a biological method of controlling the grubs of Japanese beetles. A recently introduced biological control uses predatory nematodes that you spray over the lawn. These beneficial (to humans) parasites kill grubs, cutworms, and other pests. Some pesticides are made of plant-derived poisons: sabadilla (derived from the seeds of a South American plant) is effective against chinch bugs, and rotenone is used to control billbugs and other pests.

Although these products are less toxic and less persistent in the environment than chemical sprays, use them with care, as they are poisons. Insecticides, whether botanical or synthetic in origin, should be used only as a last resort. They destroy beneficial as well as harmful insects and other creatures. Synthetic or "chemical" pesticides remain active in the environment for a longer period of time than plant-derived products.

The major diseases (including fairy ring, brown patch, leaf spot, and melting-out) that affect lawns are caused by various fungi. While applying the correct fungicide for the specific fungus afflicting your lawn may temporarily control or at least slow the spread of such diseases, proper maintenance practices are a better long-term solution. These include fertilizing at the correct time for the type of grass you have, dethatching when necessary (see page 72), and watering deeply. Letting the grass dry somewhat between irrigations is especially helpful—grass that is constantly wet is more prone to disease.

A popular approach to pest and disease control that uses fewer chemicals than traditional methods is known as Integrated Pest Management. For more information on this preventive style of pest control, see pages 94–95.

Renovating Lawns

*T*he term "renovating" covers a number of ways, beyond basic maintenance, to rejuvenate your lawn, improving its appearance and health.

▼ Dethatching

Thatch is a layer of dead roots, stems, stolons, and rhizomes that accumulates between the soil surface and the blades of grass. Unlike grass clippings, which decay quickly, thatch contains high levels of lignin, a somewhat woody material that decomposes slowly. Kentucky bluegrass, hybrid Bermuda grass, and zoysia tend to build up thatch faster than tall fescues or perennial ryegrass. A shallow layer of thatch—less than 1/2 inch—acts as a natural mulch, but a thicker layer causes problems, preventing water from reaching the soil and becoming a hiding place for insects and disease-causing fungi. Poke your fingers into the thatch to gauge its thickness.

Dethatch warm-season grasses in late spring and cool-season grasses in fall, at least a month before heavy frost, or early in spring. To do this, the soil should be moist but not wet.

You can dethatch a small lawn with a heavy rake, but a power dethatching machine (also called a vertical cutter) is more efficient. If you rent a machine, be sure the vertical cutter blades are adjusted for the kind of grass you have. For tough grasses, like Bermuda grass, the blades should be only an inch apart and set to cut through the thatch plus an inch or so into the soil. More fragile grasses, such as Bahia grass and St. Augustine grass, require a higher setting with the blades 3 inches apart.

Make several passes at right angles across your lawn to thoroughly loosen the thatch. After dethatching, rake up the debris. Add it to a compost pile along with green matter or some high nitrogen fertilizer.

▼ Aeration

The soil under lawns that receive heavy foot traffic becomes compacted, restricting the movement of air, water, and nutrients and leading to increased buildup of thatch. Aeration, also known as coring, involves punching 2- to 4-inch-deep holes into the soil at regular intervals. Use a foot-press aerator or a power model. Aerating is best done at the same time of year as dethatching.

After aerating is an ideal time to topdress the lawn, spreading a 1/8- to 1/4-inch layer of screened compost or a mixture of sand and compost (available from landscape supply firms) to add nutrients and improve drainage. Be sure to water well after aerating and topdressing.

▼ A Major Overhaul

A lawn that has become very weedy or consists of more bare patches than grass may need a complete renovation. Try to renovate cool-season grasses in early fall and warm-season grasses in spring. If there are many grassy and broad-leaved weeds in the lawn, dig them out or spray with a nonselective herbicide, following directions carefully. Then use a dethatching machine to vertically cut the remaining sod and thatch. Rake out all of the loose thatch, sod, and grass. (Don't compost these materials if you used herbicides.) Now aerate the soil as just described. Smooth out any high or low spots in the lawn.

At this time test the soil to determine if the pH needs correcting; then till or dig in lime or sulfur and a 7-21-7 fertilizer if needed. Next, sow seed, put in plugs or sprigs, or lay sod, as for a new lawn. Keep moist until the new grass is established.

Maintaining Prairies and Meadows

Once established, prairies need only an annual burning (if permitted) or mowing to slow the spread of unwanted woody plants. Mow a path to allow access to desirable prairie plants during the growing season.

Once established (about three years after planting), meadows and prairies need very little maintenance. However, before they fill in, fast-growing weeds will compete with your desired plants for water and space. They can also cast too much shade over smaller prairie plants, which need lots of sunlight to grow. For the first two years, pull out weeds as soon as they are recognizable.

For a large prairie or meadow it's easier, though less precise, to mow two or three times during the growing season the first year after planting and once the second year (in late spring) to cut down annual weeds before they grow too large or set seed. Mow, clip, or scythe at a height of 6 to 12 inches to cut above the tops of the young wildflowers and take off the seed-bearing tops of the taller weedy annuals.

Meadow and prairie plantings require little water. If rainfall is scarce, some supplemental irrigation may be needed the first summer. Be sure to water any new plants added to fill in empty spots.

Once your meadow or prairie has filled in and is growing well, the only maintenance task is annual burning or mowing. Prairie plants are adapted to a natural cycle that includes fire. Burning stops the spread of woody plants, reduces the buildup of dead leaves and stems, and induces germination of some native wildflower seeds. The best time to burn is early spring, when most of the plants are still dormant. You may need a special permit to burn your prairie—check with the local fire department. Make sure there are safe fire breaks around the burn area, such as wide paths, roads, or irrigated lawn, and have helpers on hand with garden hoses. If burning is not permitted, mowing and raking in early spring will help control the buildup of debris. Mow meadows, too, in late fall or early spring.

CHAPTER 4

Maintaining Ground Covers & Vines

a major advantage of ground covers and vines is that they require much less maintenance than lawns. • While lawns will suffer if neglected even for a week or two, ground covers and vines generally require attention only a few times each year. • When you give these low-maintenance plants some basic care—watering, fertilizing, grooming, and pruning—they reward you by becoming long-lasting and attractive additions to your landscape.

Maintaining Ground Covers

*P*roducing terrific results with ground-cover plants requires very little care. With a few simple maintenance tasks, your plants will remain healthy and productive. The following pages show how easy it is to care for ground covers.

▼ Watering, Mulching, and Weeding
Newly planted ground covers need to be watered frequently until their roots are well established in the soil. This can take one to two years. Once established, however, the different species of ground covers vary widely in their need for supplemental water. Even in areas of frequent rainfall, plants such as hostas, pachysandras, and mosses may need some summer irrigation, while junipers, rock rose *(Cistus* spp.), and thyme *(Thymus* spp.) may survive with little or no watering even in arid climates.

In addition to the ground-cover species and your climate, the type of soil in your garden affects the plants' need for water. Clay soil holds moisture around the plants' roots for a long period, but in sandy soil water quickly drains past the roots, so they require more frequent irrigation. As with lawns and other plants, it's important to water thoroughly when you do irrigate, moistening the entire root zone. Frequent light waterings encourage plants to grow shallow roots, making them more susceptible to damage from hot sun and drought.

For very small areas, such as ground covers planted between paving stones, hand watering with a hose may be sufficient. But a hose-end sprinkler, an underground sprinkler system, or a drip-irrigation system is

The downy leaves of the ground-cover plant lady's-mantle (Alchemilla vulgaris) *have a charming way of displaying drops of rain or dew.*

1 *Vigorous ground covers, like this ivy, can quickly grow out of bounds. Cut back with hedge shears.*

2 *Rake up the clippings. They can be composted, though the woody stems will take time to break down.*

3 *Ivy leaves grow quickly. The cut ends will soon be covered with new growth.*

Maintaining Ground Covers CONTINUED

Maintaining Ornamental Grasses

Ornamental grasses grown as ground-cover plantings are not entirely maintenance-free. Most species must be cut back almost to the ground once a year to get rid of old dead growth and make the plants tidier. Cut back grasses in early spring just as new growth is beginning. For large plantings, use a string trimmer or a weed trimmer with a saw blade attachment, which gives a cleaner cut. Mulch between the clumps of grass in order to prevent weeds from germinating.

more efficient for a larger area. While sprinklers work well for closely spaced ground covers, like ivy (*Hedera* spp.) or periwinkle *(Vinca* spp.), drip systems are more appropriate for widely spaced shrubby ground covers, such as creeping juniper *(Juniperus horizontalis)* and salal *(Gaultheria shallon).* Drip systems save water and are effective for slopes, since there is no evaporation or runoff. Water is delivered almost directly to the desired plants, preventing weeds from germinating and growing in the dry, unirrigated spaces. These systems are not difficult to install. Starter kits are available, and most nurseries or home improvement centers can help you choose a system and provide some tips on installing it.

Mulching immediately after planting ground covers is essential to conserve moisture and suppress weeds. It's a good idea to replenish the mulch periodically if it becomes thin over time. Organic mulches, such as crumbled compost, shredded bark, or pine needles, will improve the soil as they decompose.

Pull out any weeds that grow through the mulch. Weeds will rob your ground cover of water and nutrients, and if left too long they can take over the garden, become difficult to eradicate, and spoil the appearance of the planting.

▼ Fertilizing

Many ground covers—especially shrubby types that are drought tolerant, such as bearberry *(Arctostaphylos uva-ursi)*, rock roses *(Cistus* spp.), dwarf coyote brush *(Baccharis pilularis)*, and thyme *(Thymus* spp.)—need little or no fertilizer. On the other hand, most perennial ground covers do need a yearly feeding for best performance; these include bugleweed *(Ajuga* spp.), wild ginger *(Asarum* spp.), ivy, pachysandra, hosta, and many others. Also,

ground covers grown in competition with trees or shrubs or in sandy soil that lets nutrients quickly leach away will need more fertilizer than those planted in clay soil that holds substantial amounts of nutrients. Fertilize in early spring just before new growth begins.

As with lawns, a slow-release fertilizer, organic or synthetic, provides a steady diet for ground covers. Choose a formula that is balanced between the three major nutrients (nitrogen, phosphorous, and potassium), for example, a 10-10-10 fertilizer, which has equal amounts of the three. Such fertilizers are available in dry granular or powdered form. Apply the fertilizer at the rate indicated on the label, scattering it around the plants and scratching it in lightly with a hoe or cultivator. Then water well.

1 *A fast way to trim most low ground covers is with a lawn mower. Here ivy receives a trim.*

A path of paving bricks edged with wood both enhances and restrains the vigorous ground cover dead nettle (Lamium maculatum 'Album').

Liquid fertilizers are another option, providing nutrients quickly. These are sold either as concentrated solutions or dry concentrates that you mix with water and spray on the foliage and soil. They can also be applied efficiently through a drip-irrigation system.

▼ Pruning

Early spring is the best time to prune or cut back ground covers because new growth will quickly hide the cut branches. Heavy pruning in late summer or fall is not recommended, as the plant may then send out growth that won't have time to harden off before winter arrives, and the tender new shoots may suffer frost damage.

Basic pruning of ground covers involves taking out dead, damaged, or overcrowded branches. Some shrubby ground covers, such as cotoneasters and junipers, also need occasional shaping, since they may send out upright growing stems that spoil the horizontal look of the planting. Cut selected crowded upright branches back to the base or to a point where they meet a lateral branch or the main trunk.

Many of the low-growing, spreading ground covers need a more drastic trimming every few years to keep them neat and compact. Plants like ivy, periwinkle, yarrow *(Achillea* spp.*)*, Aaron's-beard *(Hypericum calycinum)*, pachysandra, and euonymus tend to become rangy and untidy over time. In early spring, before growth begins, mow them with a rotary mower set at its highest setting, or use a string trimmer or hedge shears. Rake up the clippings. Fertilize, mulch, and water the area; it will be bare for a few weeks, but fresh, vigorous new growth will soon appear.

Because ground-cover plants spread rapidly into new territory, it is often necessary to restrain excessive growth. Ground covers that spread by stems that root when they touch soil or by underground stems can be kept in bounds by trimming the edges of the planting with hand pruners, hedge shears, or a rotary mower, if you do it frequently. However, if the rooted stems spread too far, which often happens before you know it, use a shovel or sharp spade to dig out plants that are beyond the designated edge. Installing a permanent barrier made of brick, stones, or concrete will save a great deal of hand edging.

Maintaining Vines

Training Vines as Ground Cover

Many ground-covering vines spread out naturally, but others need training to spread evenly. Use 6-inch wire staples or rocks to direct growth, especially to encourage vines to grow uphill to cover a slope. It also helps to cut back extra-long stems to force side branching for a thicker, more even cover. Untangle branches occasionally and thin out branches that are overcrowded. As the vines mature, trim them now and then to keep them in bounds and prevent them from climbing nearby trees or shrubs.

Like ground covers, vines are easy to care for. Make sure newly planted perennial and woody vines don't dry out. They may need watering two or three times a week during their first summer. After their roots are established, most vines require an inch of water each week during the growing season, either from rainfall or irrigation. Pay special attention to vines planted under eaves, which block rain. Vines planted to climb on trees or shrubs may require extra water to make up for competition from the host plant. A few vines, notably bougainvillea, wisteria, and Cape honeysuckle *(Tecomaria capensis)*, are quite drought tolerant and do well with irrigation once a month. Most annual vines, such as sweet pea *(Lathyrus odoratus)* and morning-glory *(Ipomoea tricolor)*, need at least an inch of water a week; fast-growing gourds, such as *Cucurbita pepo* var. *ovifera* and *Lagenaria siceraria*, can use even more.

A drip-irrigation system (see pages 76–78) works well in some situations—for example, for vines along a wall. In these cases you can also use a soaker hose or hose-end sprinkler. For single vines, set a hose to drip water slowly around the base.

A 2- to 3-inch layer of mulch helps conserve moisture around vine roots and suppress weeds. Don't place mulch on the crown of the plant; it can encourage the plant to rot at the base. In cold-winter areas, add another inch or two of mulch in late fall to help protect the roots from frost damage and also prevent alternate freezing and thawing, which can heave roots out of the soil.

Most vines should be fertilized at least once a year, in early spring, just as new growth begins. Climbing roses benefit from an additional feeding in early summer. Use a balanced all-purpose fertilizer at the rate the label directs. Scratch the fertilizer into the top

A medley of well-grown vines, including Heavenly Blue morning-glory (Ipomoea tricolor) *and hyacinth bean* (Dolichos lablab), *provides a colorful backdrop for other plants.*

layer of soil, and water well. Keep an eye out for any special needs. For example, if a wisteria isn't blooming, one cause may be too much nitrogen. In this case, use a fertilizer with little or no nitrogen.

Annual vines grow quickly and do best if fertilized monthly. Use a natural fertilizer, such as fish emulsion, or one intended for vegetables.

1 To hide the bare base of a vine, like this sweet autumn clematis, use several lower-growing plants in front.

2 Start with a low shrub or perennial, such as hibiscus, positioning it immediately in front of the vine.

3 Prepare a planting hole, amending the soil with compost and taking care not to damage the roots of the vine. Plant the hibiscus.

4 To complete the camouflage, add another, lower layer of plants (here, Clara Curtis chrysanthemums). Water all the plants well.

Training Vines

Helping Reluctant Climbers

Some plants can be grown as climbers that don't actually climb readily themselves. These include climbing roses, some jasmines, and bougainvillea. To train these vines to cover an arbor, trellis, or post, tie them to the support (or to nails driven into the support) as they grow, or weave the stems through wire supports. Such vines may also scramble through other plants, once headed in the right direction.

Special vine clips or masonry hooks (available at hardware stores and nurseries) are useful for training any of the climbers that don't have aerial roots or discs to a brick wall. Insert the hooks into the mortar, then thread the stems through the hooks or clips.

*T*rain vines to grow where you want them as soon as they are planted. If allowed to sprawl, the young stems quickly become tangled, and they are difficult to separate without breaking. Also, young stems are flexible and easier to train than brittle older stems.

The first step in training climbing vines is to lead the stems to their support. If the trellis or other support is higher than the young stems, drive short stakes into the ground leading to the support and tie the stems to these stakes with soft twine or plastic tape. Always tie stems loosely enough that growth will not be constricted, and check them periodically.

The delicate stem of a morning-glory climbs upward around stretched twine. Twining vines will climb best on slender vertical supports.

Vines that cling or hold on with aerial roots or adhesive discs (sticky pads that form at the tips of some plants' aerial roots) need little training once they start up a wall or fence. Some, such as climbing hydrangea *(H. anomala* subsp. *petiolaris)*, may not grow strong holdfasts until they are a couple of years old. Tie the stems to a temporary wire support to help them begin their climb.

Most twining vines are best trained on wires or fairly narrow posts. To get a twiner, such as wisteria, to twist around a stout support like the post of an arbor, select a main stem, cutting away others, and tie it to the post every foot or so with plastic tape or stronger insulated wire. Remove the ties once the vine is holding on by itself. To train a twiner to grow on a trellis, chain-link fence, twine, or vertical wires, fan out the stems and gently weave them through the trellis or twist them around the twine or wires. Repeat this every few weeks to direct the growth evenly. If the vine has only a single stem, prune it back above several strong buds to force the growth of lateral shoots, which can then be trained onto the support.

Vines that climb by grabbing onto supports with tendrils, such as grape *(Vitis* spp.*)*, clematis, cross vine *(Bignonia* spp.*)*, passionflower *(Passiflora* spp.*)*, and porcelain berry *(Ampelopsis)*, also need some initial training. Choose a main stem and tie it to the post of an arbor every foot or so as it ascends. Vines with tendrils will cover a bare fence or trellis more effectively if given horizontal as well as vertical wires to hold onto.

1 *The photos on this page show various supports for vines. A simple tepee and string structure supports scarlet runner beans.*

2 *Use a clamp made especially for vines to help trumpet creeper (Campsis radicans) hold on to a masonry wall.*

3 *English ivy (Hedera helix) can climb any wall by means of its aerial roots ("holdfasts"), which burrow into tiny holes or cracks in the masonry.*

4 *Guide the twining stems of morning-glory (Ipomoea tricolor) to cover a picket fence.*

5 *Train clematis to grow up and through a trellis while the stems are young and flexible.*

6 *Fasten wires or strings vertically to the uprights of an arbor for morning-glories to climb.*

Training Vines CONTINUED

1 Prepare the site for a new arbor by removing weeds, leveling the soil, and spreading mulch evenly across the site.

2 Mark the arbor dimensions by laying boards on the ground. Check that the diagonal measurements are equal to ensure square corners.

3 Mark the location where the center of each post or upright should be. With a post-hole digger, dig a 3-foot-deep hole for each post.

4 Use a spirit level to make sure the posts are at a 90-degree angle from the ground. Check all sides of the posts.

5 Secure the crosspieces with nails or bolts, checking that they are level and that they are evenly spaced apart.

6 Use fast-growing annual vines, such as calabash gourds (Lagenaria siceraria), to decorate the arbor while slower permanent vines get started.

Pruning Vines

Vines generally need some pruning each year—more for vigorous well-established vines, less for young vines and those that remain small naturally. Basically, pruning is done to direct growth where you want it, to control or thin excess growth, and in many vines, to promote the growth of shoots that will produce flowers. To decide when and how often to prune, you must consider the kind of vine—whether it is woody or tender, whether the vine grows quickly or slowly, or whether it is grown for its foliage or flowers. Certain vines, such as clematis and roses, require a little extra knowledge when it comes to pruning (see pages 88–89).

Climbing roses respond with increased flowering to regular maintenance, including mulching, watering, fertilizing, and once established, annual pruning.

▼ Pruning Woody Vines

As a general guideline, remove dead, damaged, or diseased wood first on woody vines, cutting back to live growth. Then take out tangled or congested growth. Tie the remaining stems to the support, if necessary, or weave them into their trellis or fence. Make pruning cuts just above a bud that faces the direction you want a new shoot to grow. Don't cut too close to or too far above the bud (aim for about ⅛ inch). Cutting too close to the bud can damage it, while a cut made too far away leaves an unattractive stub that dies back and may allow disease-causing organisms to enter. Sharp hand pruners are the tool of choice for pruning most vines, although a pair of heavier long-handled loppers may come in handy for large or older vines and shears may be useful for taking off thin shoots.

Foliage vines, such as wintercreeper (*Euonymus fortunei*), English ivy (*Hedera helix*), and Boston ivy (*Parthenocissus tricuspidata*), usually need only a trim to keep them close to the wall that supports them. They may, however, require a more severe pruning to prevent them from overtaking windows or rooftops. Prune deciduous foliage vines in winter, when their leaves have fallen. Evergreen vines should be pruned in spring or early summer, as pruning too late in the year may force new growth that doesn't have time to harden off or ripen before frost.

As with shrubs, the time of year to prune an established flowering vine depends on whether it blooms on new or old wood. Some species flower on the new or current season's growth—that is, shoots that grew since winter from dormant buds. (See the sidebar on page 86 for vines that grow this way.) These are best pruned in winter or early spring, just before new growth begins. How much to prune depends on the species of vine and how you want it to grow.

Pruning Vines CONTINUED

Vines That Bloom on New Wood

Climbing vines that flower on new or the current season's growth and therefore should be pruned in late winter include trumpet creeper (Campsis radicans), *honeysuckles* (Lonicera spp.), *mandevilla species, blue passionflower* (Passiflora caerulea) *and maypop* (P. incarnata), *silver lace vine* (Polygonum aubertii), *potato vine* (Solanum jasminoides) *and blue potato vine* (S. crispum), *Madagascar jasmine* (Stephanotis floribunda), *and grapes* (Vitis spp.).

Vigorous vines, like trumpet creeper *(Campsis radicans)* or potato vine *(Solanum jasminoides)*, may need to be cut back severely to keep them in bounds in a small garden. In a large garden a lighter trimming of last year's growth to promote new shoots for this year's flowers will suffice. Wayward or extra-long shoots can be cut back until midsummer, and new shoots should be tied to the support if necessary.

Other vine species flower on old wood—shoots that grew during the previous summer. (See the sidebar on page 87 for examples.) Pruning in winter or spring removes many of those shoots, so there will be few flowers. Instead, prune such vines right after they bloom, in early to late spring, depending on the species. This gives the vine time to grow over summer and lets new shoots ripen before winter. After removing deadwood, cut back stems that have flowered to vigorous new shoots; also remove any tangled or congested growth.

Most vines that naturally grow quite vigorously can, if necessary, be cut back to within a foot or so of the ground and will regrow in a few years. This type of renewal pruning may be needed if the vine has become too overgrown and tangled to prune any other way, or in order to repair or paint its support. This treatment works well with honeysuckles *(Lonicera spp.)*, porcelain berry *(Ampelopsis brevipedunculata)*, golden-trumpet vine *(Allamanda cathartica)*, and silver lace vine *(Polygonum aubertii)*, among others, but isn't a good idea with wisteria, which takes too long to grow back and bloom again. Sometimes frost-tender vines, such as potato vine or jasmine, are badly damaged during an unusually cold winter; it's worth cutting out the dead growth and waiting to see whether they may sprout again from the roots.

Wisteria requires little care other than regular pruning to produce its wonderful springtime display.

▼ Pruning Clematis

Prune clematis vines according to when they bloom. They are usually divided into three main groups, based on growth habit and flowering time: early-flowering, spring-blooming, and summer-blooming species.

1 Once it reaches flowering size, wisteria requires regular pruning to keep it in bounds. In early summer, after blossoming, cut back long, whippy stems.

2 Remove offshoots or suckers growing at the base; if these come from the rootstock of a grafted vine, they can crowd out the selected top part.

Vines That Bloom on Old Wood

Climbers that flower on wood that grew the previous summer are best pruned soon after blooming. These include vines in the genus Actinidia, *such as hardy kiwi* (A. arguta) *and* A. kolomikta, *golden-trumpet vine* (Allamanda cathartica), *bougainvillea, Carolina yellow jessamine* (Gelsemium sempervirens), *climbing hydrangea* (H. anomala *subsp.* petiolaris), *jasmine* (Jasminum *spp.*), *the tender bower vine* (Pandorea jasminoides), *Japanese hydrangea vine* (Schizophragma hydrangeoides), *and wisteria.*

3 Cut back dense foliage to thin the plant and let in light. This may stimulate repeat blooming in late summer.

4 Thin the branches a bit more if you wish to reveal a handsome building facade behind the vine.

Pruning Vines CONTINUED

TROUBLESHOOTING TIP

There are several ways to encourage a wisteria to bloom. When you buy a wisteria, be sure it was grown from a cutting or is grafted—those grown from seed may take many more years to bloom. Let it get plenty of sun. After the vine has been in the ground for a few years, give it less water and nitrogen fertilizer. Prune carefully to cut down on leafy growth and encourage flowering.

If an established vine refuses to bloom, try withholding all nitrogen fertilizer for one growing season and applying superphosphate instead. If that doesn't help, prune the vine's roots late the next spring. To do this, force a spade into the soil in a circle 1½ feet from the trunk, cutting the lateral roots.

The first group, early-flowering species, includes anemone clematis *(C. montana* and its cultivars*)* and evergreen clematis *(C. armandii).* These vigorous vines need little pruning unless they become overgrown and tangled. Since they produce flowers on old wood, do any necessary pruning soon after flowering is finished; this allows the plant time to grow and stems to ripen for flowering next year. Evergreen clematis often becomes overgrown and top-heavy; it looks best with an annual thinning.

The second group of clematis are the large-flowered hybrids that bloom in spring, including C. 'Henryi', C. 'Nelly Moser', and C. 'The President'. Their beautiful flowers are produced on shoots that grow from last season's stems—thus, they bloom on a combination of old and new wood. Prune these in early spring, just before new growth begins, taking out dead or damaged growth and, if desired, cutting back healthy stems to just above a pair of leaf buds. These buds will soon send out shoots and flowers. Often this group of clematis will bloom again in late summer on new stems.

The third group, including Florida clematis *(C. florida),* sweet autumn clematis *(C. paniculata),* and golden clematis *(C. tangutica),* blooms from midsummer to fall on the current season's growth. Prune these in early spring, before new growth begins, cutting all of last year's stems back to 1 to 1½ feet above the base of the plant; make cuts above a strong pair of leaf buds.

▼ **Pruning Climbing Roses**
Climbing roses are best left unpruned for the first two or three years after planting, removing only dead or

1 *Prune early-blooming clematis, such as C. montana, soon after flowering is finished. Cut back wayward stems.*

2 *When cutting off excess growth, make each cut to just above a pair of leaves.*

weak growth. This gives the plants time to become established and produce the long canes (stems) that will form the framework of the plant. As these canes grow, train them to their support, tying them with twine or strips of soft cloth. First tie the twine firmly around the support, then loop it loosely around the rose cane, taking care not to constrict its growth.

Climbing roses produce their blossoms on lateral branches that grow from the main canes. More of these lateral branches—and therefore more flowers—will develop if the canes are trained horizontally (for example, along a fence or tied sideways on a trellis). Gently bend and tie the canes to grow horizontally as they reach the desired height.

Generally, climbing roses bloom with little pruning. However, once the rose has reached more or less full size, you can encourage more vigorous flowering by pruning back the laterals growing on the main canes. In early spring, just as new growth begins, cut back the stems, leaving three or four buds. Also shorten any canes that are growing beyond their support. Removing spent blossoms later in the season will help stimulate everblooming climbers to flower again.

As the vine ages, occasional renewal pruning will keep it vigorous. This is best done in early spring. Thin out the oldest canes—those that are no longer producing flowering laterals—to make room for new canes to grow. Cut off the old canes close to the ground with long-handled loppers or a pruning saw. As new canes grow, tie them to the support.

Pruning Rambler Roses

Ramblers are climbing roses that produce clusters of blossoms in late spring or early summer on one-year-old wood. Examples include 'Dorothy Perkins', 'Crimson Rambler', and 'Excelsa'.

After flowering, ramblers develop many new canes from the base; these will bear next year's blossoms. This growth can become a tangled mess if left unpruned for many years.

Prune ramblers in summer, just after they finish blooming. Cut about one-third of the oldest canes back to the ground. Also shorten any shoots growing out of bounds.

Fasten the remaining canes to a fence or trellis.

1 *Rampant growth of sweet autumn clematis can be cut back at any time, but it's best to prune it in early spring.*

2 *Separate and prune long, tangled vine stems. Cut them back to within a foot or so of the base of the plant.*

Propagation

*P*ropagation is the art and science of starting new plants. Described here are vegetative means of propagating plants—dividing, taking cuttings, and layering—which result in plants that are identical to the parent plant (unlike those grown from seed). Learning to propagate new plants from those you already have allows you to increase the size of a ground-cover planting at little cost. It also may be the only way to get more plants of a rare climbing rose or other vine. Note that many ground covers and vines can be propagated by more than one means.

Division is the easiest way to increase the many ground-cover plants that grow in spreading clumps or expand by sending out stolons or rhizomes. Such ground covers include bugleweed *(Ajuga* spp.), daylilies *(Hemerocallis* spp.), dead nettle *(Lamium*

spp.*)*, foamflower *(Tiarella cordifolia)*, hosta, hypericum, lamb's-ears *(Stachys byzantina)*, lily-of-the-valley *(Convallaria majalis)*, pachysandra, and most ornamental grasses.

Division is best done in early spring in cold climates, to give new plants plenty of time to become established before freezing weather. In milder climates you can divide ground covers in either early spring or fall. Before digging up the parents, prepare the new planting area, removing weeds and tilling in organic matter and fertilizer. Or prepare a temporary nursery bed for the divisions until you are ready to put them in their permanent home.

If the soil is dry, irrigate a day or two before dividing plants. Dig up clumps or sections of the ground cover and pull them apart into separate small plants, each with some roots and stems (or buds that will

A mixed planting of lily-of-the-valley (Convallaria majalis) *and pachysandra carpets the ground. Both of these plants are easily increased by division.*

1 *Crowded stoloniferous ground covers are ready to be divided. This foamflower (Tiarella cordifolia) planting is ready for division.*

2 *Dig up a clump of foamflowers, and divide it into individual small plants or offsets, making sure each one has its own healthy root.*

3 *Plant the offsets in flats to grow strong roots. If divisions are already well rooted, you can plant them directly in the garden.*

grow into stems). Replant without delay, and keep the new planting well watered.

To extend a planting of mat-forming ground covers, it's easier to transplant clumps several inches in diameter than to separate out smaller divisions. Plant the chunks in well-prepared soil, and fill the holes in the original planting with a mixture of compost and soil to help the remaining plants fill in again. Yarrow (*Achillea* spp.), wild thyme (*Thymus serpyllum*), blue star creeper (*Laurentia fluviatilis*), and mosses all respond well to this treatment.

Cuttings take more effort than division, but you can make many more new plants using stems from only one or two mother plants. Softwood cuttings, which are made in summer, are an excellent way to propagate many woody ground covers and vines, including cotoneaster, English ivy (*Hedera helix*), pachysandra, santolina, creeping rosemary (*Rosmarinus officinalis* 'Prostratus'), clematis, Boston ivy (*Parthenocissus tricuspidata*), Virginia creeper (*P.*

quinquefolia), honeysuckle (*Lonicera* spp.), potato vine (*Solanum jasminoides*), roses, and wisteria.

Clean containers, such as 6-inch plastic pots or flats, and fill with light potting mix—equal parts moist peat moss and perlite is a good choice, as it drains easily yet holds enough moisture.

Take the cuttings in the morning. Cut healthy stems that are green and flexible, avoiding very thin or weak twigs and unusually fat stems. Using a sharp knife, cut off and discard any side branches, flower buds, or fruits; also discard the soft tip of each stem. Then cut the remaining stem into 3- to 4-inch-long pieces, each with at least two nodes or growing points. Make the bottom cut on each piece just below a node, which is where the new roots will grow. Strip the leaves off the lower half of the cutting.

Dip the bottom of the cutting in rooting hormone powder, tapping off any excess. Then make holes in the rooting medium with a pencil, spacing them far enough apart so that the leaves of the cuttings will

Propagation CONTINUED

barely touch. Insert each cutting, firming the medium around it. Water immediately and label each pot with the name of the plant and the date.

To minimize moisture loss, cover each pot with a clear plastic bag. Ventilate this mini-greenhouse a few minutes each day to prevent rotting.

Place the cuttings in bright but indirect light. Most plants take four to eight weeks to root well; when they have rooted, new leaves will appear. Gradually expose them to drier air by slicing open the bag, a little more each day. When they seem strong enough, transplant the rooted cuttings to individual pots, keeping them shaded and well watered. Place them in a cold frame during winter, and set them in the garden when they are about a year old.

Layering is a propagation method that takes advantage of the natural tendency of many woody ground covers and vines to form roots and produce new plants wherever their trailing stems touch the ground. Under the edges of a planting of English ivy, winter-creeper *(Euonymus fortunei)*, climbing fig *(Ficus pumila)*, or star jasmine *(Trachelospermum jasminoides)*, you may discover self-layered shoots; if these are growing well, you can sever them from the parent plant and transplant them to a new area.

Transplant self-layered shoots in spring or early fall, when the weather is mild. Prepare the new planting area, as for divisions, so the rooted shoots won't have to risk dehydration. Or transplant the new plants to pots or a nursery bed, letting them grow a bit before moving them to a permanent spot. Cut the new plant from the parent, and with a small shovel or hand fork dig carefully around it, lifting as much of the root ball as possible. After replanting, water well.

Honeysuckle (Lonicera *spp.*) *is easy to propagate from cuttings. Other vines propagated this way include clematis,* English ivy (Hedera helix), *Boston ivy* (Parthenocissus tricuspidata), *Virginia creeper* (P. quinquefolia), *and climbing roses.*

1 To make softwood cuttings of a vine such as the clematis shown here, cut the stems into 3- to 4-inch pieces, each with at least two leaf nodes.

2 Dip the bottom end in rooting hormone and insert it into a flat of rooting medium and water. Cover with plastic and place in indirect light.

Serial Layering

Also called serpentine layering, this technique allows you to start several new plants at one time from one long shoot. Prepare the soil under the shoot by digging in compost. Trim off leaves and side shoots at several points along the stem, leaving at least one set of leaves between each trimmed area. Make notches on the underside of the stem at the trimmed areas and treat with rooting hormone powder. Fasten down the wounded sections in small holes, and cover with soil. Transplant when the new plants are well rooted.

You can encourage many ground covers and vines to layer, even if they haven't done so naturally. In addition to the plants mentioned above, you can do this with trumpet creeper *(Campsis radicans)*, honeysuckle, jasmine *(Jasminum* spp.*)*, passionflower *(Passiflora* spp.*)*, potato vine, Boston ivy, Virginia creeper, wisteria, Scotch heather *(Calluna vulgaris)*, heaths *(Erica* spp.*)*, partridgeberry *(Mitchella repens)*, and santolina.

Start the layering process in spring—newly rooted plants will be ready to transplant in fall or, for slower-rooting species, by the next spring. If the soil surrounding the parent plant is poor, incorporate a few inches of compost. Choose a healthy, flexible stem long enough to lay easily on the ground. Prepare a section to layer, about 8 to 12 inches back from the tip of the stem, by trimming off any leaves and side branches. Dig a shallow hole under the stem, and gently bend the trimmed area into the hole. Hold it in place with a U-shaped wire, and cover the stem with a couple of inches of soil, leaving the tip of the shoot free. Plants with woody stems often form roots more quickly if you have wounded the stem before burying it. To do this, use a sharp knife and cut a notch halfway through the underside of the stem. Apply rooting hormone powder to the wound with a clean brush, shaking off any excess. Peg down and bury the stem.

Tying the tip of the stem to a stake will help hold the layer in place and remind you of its location. Apply a shallow layer of mulch, and keep the area moist. New growth coming from the tip indicates that rooting has taken place and that you can cut the new plant from the parent and transplant it.

Managing Pests and Diseases

A healthy garden is a habitat for diverse species of plants, birds, small mammals, reptiles, and various insects. In such a habitat a natural system of checks and balances evolves that usually works to keep the garden healthy. As part of this system, many insects that are potentially harmful to plants are kept in check by predatory insects and other creatures. Indiscriminate spraying of pesticides (including herbicides and fungicides) can upset this system by destroying the beneficial creatures along with harmful ones.

Integrated pest management (IPM) is an ecologically based approach to pest and disease control that emphasizes the concept of a garden as a functioning system or habitat. IPM helps you choose the least harmful strategies—to you and the environment— that will solve your pest problems.

IPM begins with the idea of using practices that enhance the overall health of the garden and thus help make it a balanced system. Choose plants that are well adapted to your climate and resistant to pests and diseases known to be present in your area— checking with knowledgeable nursery personnel and local gardeners for this sort of information *before* planting can save a lot of future worries about pests and diseases. For example, if fire blight (a bacterial disease that causes twigs to blacken and die suddenly) is common among cotoneaster and its relatives, such as pyracantha, in your region, choose ground covers from a different plant family. Plants should also be adapted to specific microclimates in your garden; placing a shade-loving plant in sun is asking for trouble—it will be stressed and therefore more susceptible to pests and disease.

Keep the garden clean to help prevent pests and disease organisms from breeding or overwintering in plant debris. And remove any diseased or dead plant parts to avoid the spread of pests and diseases.

Under the IPM philosophy, mechanical or physical controls are the safest and therefore the first line of defense when problems do occur. Handpicking and destroying insects, while not a particularly enjoyable pastime, can significantly reduce the population of slugs, snails, and some beetles. Traps that target many insects are available. Homemade traps for snails and slugs can be very effective. A wide board elevated an inch off the ground provides a daytime "hiding" place for these pests, so you can easily find and destroy them. To keep snails and slugs away from plants in containers, wrap copper bands around the outside of the pot; the pests will not cross this barrier. You can dislodge many small insects, such as aphids, from plants by using a strong spray of water from a garden hose. In addition, insecticidal soap is effective against aphids, spider mites, scale insects, and rose slugs, as well as a number of other pests. Be sure to test it on a few leaves before spraying a ground-cover planting or a vine, as the leaves of some plants are harmed by the soap.

Biological controls are the next step in controlling pests. Because these controls are, for the most part, specific to certain pests, you should correctly identify the pest before using them. To do this, take a few of the suspect insects as well as a sample of the damaged plants to your county cooperative extension agent or a local nursery.

Biological controls include releasing into your garden beneficial nematodes or helpful insects such as ladybugs and trichogramma wasps. These are all natural predators of harmful insects. You can also encourage the populations of beneficial insects that may already be present in your garden by providing them with shelter—for example, a planting of tall ground covers—or food (many such insects live on plants of the parsley family, which also includes dill, fennel, and caraway). And insects, like birds and other creatures, appreciate a source of water, such as a shallow birdbath.

Another sort of biological control involves introducing diseases that affect specific insects. Milky spore disease, used to control the grubs of Japanese beetles in lawns, is a familiar example of this approach. *Bacillus thuringiensis* (Bt) is a widely used bacteria that kills caterpillars and certain other insects but does not harm other creatures.

Botanical pesticides are derived from plants that have insecticidal properties. While they are less harmful to the user and the environment than synthesized chemical sprays, they do kill many organisms besides the target pest. However, they are quickly broken down into harmless by-products by sunlight and are therefore short-lived in the environment. Neem is the newest of the botanicals, at least in this country. Made from the seeds of the tropical neem tree, it is effective against many common insects, including whiteflies, thrips, leaf miners, caterpillars, aphids, weevils, and leafhoppers. Other botanical pesticides often used for lawn pests include pyrethrin, rotenone, and sabadilla (see page 71).

A healthy canary creeper (Tropaeolum peregrinum) *joins forces with geraniums and wax begonias to brighten a fence and narrow planting bed.*

Chemical controls for insects or diseases are a last resort. Before using these be sure you have identified the problem correctly. And always read and follow the instructions on the label exactly, both to minimize harm to the environment and to help ensure the chemical will be as effective as possible.

End-of-Season Care

Ground Covers for Fall and Winter

Cotoneasters feature bright red berries that often last into winter, and in fall the foliage of the deciduous species turns red. Some varieties of wintercreeper (Euonymus fortunei) offer exceptional fall interest: The leaves of 'Colorata' turn a deep purple in fall and winter, while 'Gracilis' has attractive leaves variegated with white or cream, some of which become pink in cold weather.

The leaflets of creeping mahonia (M. repens) are purple in winter, and the dark blue berries may remain through winter.

Sweet autumn clematis (C. paniculata) *produces masses of small, white, sweetly fragrant flowers in late summer and fall.*

The distinctive fruit of porcelain berry (Ampelopsis brevipedunculata) *is turquoise at first, ripening to pinkish purple.*

Spending a little time caring for your ground-cover plants and vines during the cool days of fall will give you a healthier and more attractive garden the following year. Start by raking fallen leaves that may smother ground covers. Cut back spent growth and dead flowers. Pulling weeds now will mean fewer to contend with in spring. Remove any garden debris that may have collected around climbing roses, other vines, and ground covers, as dead plant materials lying on the ground may harbor disease organisms and insects over winter.

Fall is a good time to start a compost heap if you don't have one. Mix fallen leaves, weeds, and other garden debris with grass clippings and organic kitchen waste, such as vegetable peelings and coffee grounds, but no meat. Keep the pile moist and turn it every few weeks to speed decomposition. Don't add any plant material that appears to be diseased or weeds that have gone to seed.

Don't give plants fertilizers high in nitrogen in fall, as nitrogen will cause them to produce lush new growth that won't have time to harden before cold weather arrives.

Check your vines and tie any loose new growth to the trellis or arbor to keep the stems from being blown about and damaged by winter winds. Before the first hard frost be sure to move tender vines in containers to a protected spot. Water them as needed over winter so that they don't dry out completely.

In all areas, fall is a good time to renew mulches around ground covers and vines. Spread a 2-inch layer of ground or shredded bark or compost. In mild, rainy climates, take care not to bury the crowns of plants, which could cause them to rot. In cold cli-

The scarlet fall foliage of Virginia creeper (Parthenocissus quinquefolia) *shows up brilliantly against a wall or fence. This vine is also effective grown as a ground cover.*

The large glossy leaves of Boston ivy (Parthenocissus tricuspidata) *hang gracefully against a wall throughout the season, turning an outstanding shade of scarlet in fall.*

Vines for Fall and Winter Interest

Vines can be a colorful addition to fall gardens. For flowers, plant sweet autumn clematis (C. paniculata), golden clematis (C. tangutica), and silver lace vine (Polygonum aubertii).

Both Boston ivy (Parthenocissus tricuspidata) and Virginia creeper (P. quinquefolia) are noted for their glorious fall color. Crimson glory vine (Vitis coignetiae) has large rounded leaves that turn a brilliant scarlet in fall.

For colorful fruit, plant porcelain berry (Ampelopsis brevipedunculata), with its turquoise to deep purple fruits, or American bittersweet (Celastrus scandens).

mates an extra layer of mulch (to be removed in spring) will help protect plants from winter damage due to alternate freezing and thawing of the soil. Apply this mulch after the first hard frosts. Evergreen boughs, straw, or shredded leaves are all useful for this purpose.

Make sure the soil around evergreen plants is moist as winter arrives to help prevent desiccation of leaves during freezing weather.

In very cold climates some varieties of climbing roses, like other roses, may need extra protection to make it through winter. (Planting cultivars known to be hardy in your area saves a lot of work!) As with other plants, don't fertilize climbing roses late in the season, and be sure to keep the plants well watered until the soil freezes. After night temperatures remain below freezing, mound about a foot of soil over the base of each climber. Then wrap the canes in burlap stuffed with straw, or for even more protection, untie the canes from their support and carefully bend them to the ground. Fasten them down and cover with soil. A layer of evergreen boughs over the mounded soil will act as further insulation.

When the weather turns cool in early fall, northern gardeners should move tender perennials in containers indoors to a greenhouse or bright location to spend the winter.

Finally, when annual and tender perennial vines not being brought indoors are killed by frost, pull them up (or remove them from containers) and put them on the compost pile.

Regional Calendar of Garden Care

	🌱 *Spring*	☀ *Summer*

COOL CLIMATES

Spring
- In early spring, sow seeds of annual vines indoors.
- Gradually remove protective mulch as weather warms.
- Prune vines that flower on new wood and foliage vines.
- Cut back, or if legal, burn meadows and prairies.
- Cut back ornamental grasses.
- Fertilize lawns, ground covers, and vines. Also spread lime on lawns, if needed.
- Renovate ground covers by pruning or cutting back. Rake and weed the planting area.
- Plant ground covers, vines, and meadows.
- Divide ground covers and ornamental grasses.

Summer
- In early summer, transplant annual vines started from seed to the garden.
- Lay sod.
- Mow lawns, as needed, to the correct height for the particular grass species.
- Water lawns, ground covers, and vines as needed.
- Edge and trim ground covers.
- Train and tie up vines.
- Take cuttings of ground covers and vines.

WARM CLIMATES

Spring
- Sow seeds of annual vines indoors; hardy ones may be sown outdoors where they are to grow.
- Prune vines that flower on new wood and foliage vines.
- Cut back ornamental grasses.
- Renovate ground covers by pruning or cutting back. Rake and weed the planting area.
- Fertilize lawns, ground covers, and vines. Also spread lime on lawns, if needed.
- Dethatch and aerate lawns.
- Seed, plant sprigs or plugs, or lay sod for lawns.
- Plant ground covers and vines.
- Divide ornamental grasses. Layer vines and ground covers.

Summer
- In early summer, transplant annual vines started from seed indoors to the garden.
- Fertilize lawns.
- Mow lawns, as needed, to the correct height for the particular grass species.
- Water lawns, ground covers, and vines as needed.
- Lay sod.
- Edge and trim ground covers.
- Train and tie up vines.
- Take cuttings of ground covers and vines.

Fall

- Seed or lay sod for lawn.
- Continue to mow lawns and water all plants as needed.
- Dethatch and aerate lawns.
- Fertilize lawns.
- Clean up debris and weeds around ground covers and vines.
- Move vines in containers to a protected spot indoors.
- Prepare winter protection for climbing roses, if needed.
- After the ground freezes, add extra mulch around ground covers and vines for winter protection.

Winter

- Make notes about how your garden performed over the past year, including ideas for changes and new plantings for the future.
- Clean and repair garden tools.
- Do routine maintenance on gasoline-powered engines.
- Sharpen mower blades.
- Order seeds of annual vines from mail-order nurseries. Also order vines and ground-cover plants.
- Prune grapes in late winter before the sap rises.

This table offers a basic outline of garden care by season. The tasks for each season differ for warm and cool climates: warm climates correspond to USDA Plant Hardiness zones 8 through 11, and cool climates to zones 2 through 7. Obviously, there are substantial climate differences within these broad regions. To understand the specific growing conditions in your area, consult the Zone Map on page 127. Also be sure to study local factors affecting the microclimate of your garden, such as elevation and proximity of water.

- Plant vines and ground covers.
- Plant meadows and prairies.
- Divide ground covers.
- In mid-fall, overseed warm-season grasses with annual or perennial rye for a green lawn in winter.
- Continue to mow lawns and water all plants as needed.
- Clean up debris and weeds around ground covers and vines.
- Renew mulch around ground covers and vines.
- Tie and train vines.

- In the mildest areas, continue to plant ground covers.
- Weed and add mulch as necessary.
- Mow lawn if overseeded with rye.
- Make notes about how your garden performed over the past year, including ideas for changes and new plantings for the future.
- Clean and repair tools. Repair irrigation systems.
- Order seeds of annual vines from mail-order nurseries. Also order vines and ground covers for early spring planting.
- Prune grapes in late winter before the sap rises.

Ground Covers & Vines for American Gardens

*T*his section provides concise information on more than 130 vines and ground-cover plants. The plants have been selected on the basis of beauty, adaptability, and availability. Below are descriptions of what information each column in the encyclopedia offers.

▼ Plant Names

Plants appear in alphabetical order by the genus name, shown in bold type. On the next line is the common name. The third listing contains the complete botanical name: genus, species, and if applicable, the variety or cultivar. Occasionally an alternative botanical name is listed below this in parentheses.

Common names vary, but botanical names are the same everywhere. If you learn botanical names, you'll always get the plant you want from a mail-order nursery or local garden center. One gardener's tea-berry may be another gardener's wintergreen, but both gardeners will recognize the plant if they know its scientific name: *Gaultheria procumbens.*

In the case of a genus containing two or more different species that cannot be covered in a single entry, each of the recommended species is given a separate entry in the chart.

The second column of the chart provides a brief plant description. Look here to see if the plant is an annual or perennial; evergreen or deciduous; climbing, sprawling, or spreading.

▼ Flower Color

The color dots following each description indicate the color *family* and are not a literal rendering of the flower color. Plants with pink dots might have pale blush pink, clear pink, or bright rose pink flowers.

▼ Time of Bloom

Bloom time is given by season and may vary from one region to another according to climate, weather, and growing conditions. For example, the annual vine sweet pea *(Lathyrus odoratus)* blooms in late spring to midsummer in northern gardens but can be grown for winter flowers in warm climates.

▼ Growth Habit

A plant's mature height and spread are expressed here in ranges to account for the natural variability in plant growth. Some plants can be grown as either ground covers or vines; the heights for both forms are indicated in these cases. In addition, spacing information (how close together to plant) has been provided where applicable. Keep in mind that the distances recommended for spacing are quite general and should be adjusted to fit such gardeners' concerns as plant cost and rapidity of spread.

▼ Hardiness

Plant hardiness is generally an indication of the coldest temperatures a plant is likely to survive. But many plants also have limits to the amount of heat they can tolerate. In this chart hardiness is expressed as a range from the coolest to the warmest zones where the plant generally thrives. The zones are based on the newest version of the USDA Plant Hardiness Zone Map, shown on page 127.

▼ Growing Conditions

The last column of the chart summarizes the best growing conditions for the plant, including its light, moisture, and soil requirements.

		Flower Color	Time of Bloom	Growth Habit	Hardiness Zones	Growing Conditions
ACHILLEA WOOLLY YARROW *Achillea tomentosa*	A perennial ground cover forming a mat of ferny, deep green, aromatic leaves covered with woolly hairs. Dense, 2-in. clusters of ⅛-in. flower heads are borne above the foliage.		Early to mid-summer	Height: 6–10" Spread: 1–3' Spacing: 1–2'	4 to 10	Full sun. Well-drained soil. Tolerates hot, dry conditions; overwatering may lead to mildew problems. Achillea spreads rapidly and is a good plant for a rock garden or edging next to a walkway.
ACTINIDIA HARDY KIWI *Actinidia arguta* KOLOMIKTA ACTINIDIA *A. kolomikta*	Woody, climbing vines with 3- to 6-in., heart-shaped leaves and fragrant, ¾-in., white flowers. Delicious, 1-in.-long, fall berries look like hairless kiwifruit. The foliage of A. arguta is green; that of A. kolomikta is variegated with white or pink.	○	Mid- to late spring	A. arg. Height: 10–30' Spread: 3–5' A. kolo. Height: 10–20' Spread: 3–5'	3 to 8	Full sun to partial shade. Evenly moist, well-drained, ordinary garden soil. Both species grow rapidly and need to be pruned down to several feet tall each year. For maximum fruiting, provide trellis support for vines. Space plants 2 to 3 ft. apart.
AJUGA BUGLEWEED *Ajuga pyramidalis* CARPET BUGLEWEED *A. reptans*	Low, creeping perennial ground covers with glossy green leaves that rise 4 in. from the ground in A. reptans and 6 in. in A. pyramidalis; spikes of blue or lavender flowers rise above the foliage. Cultivars offer leaf and flower variations.	○ ◓ ●	Spring to early summer	Height: 6–10" Spread: 6–18" Spacing: 6–12"	4 to 9	Full sun to partial shade, with some afternoon shade in warm climates. Soil should not be wet or excessively drained. Bugleweed can become weedy if planted with other border or bedding plants.
ALCHEMILLA LADY'S-MANTLE *Alchemilla vulgaris* *(A. mollis)*	A low border and edging perennial with particularly attractive, scalloped, gray-green foliage. Tiny yellow-green flowers are borne in loose, spraylike clusters above the leaves.	○ ◓	Spring to midsummer	Height: 8–18" Spread: 1–2' Spacing: 6–12"	4 to 8	Full sun to partial shade. Ordinary, evenly moist garden soil, neither very wet nor very dry. Lady's-mantle can become somewhat weedy with age and may need to be divided.
ALLAMANDA GOLDEN-TRUMPET VINE *Allamanda cathartica*	A vigorously growing, tender perennial vine with pairs or whorls of 4- to 6-in.-long, lance-shaped, evergreen leaves. Fragrant, tubular, bright yellow, 5-in. flowers have paler yellow throats.		Summer to autumn	Height: 10–50' Spread: 1–2' Spacing: 1–2'	10 to 11	Full sun to light shade. Fertile, evenly moist, well-drained, humus-rich soil. Allamanda survives longest where soil is dry during the winter. Cut vines back in early spring before the start of the growing season.

Indicates species shown

Ground Covers & Vines

		Flower Color	Time of Bloom	Growth Habit	Hardiness Zones	Growing Conditions
AMPELOPSIS PEPPER VINE *Ampelopsis arborea* PORCELAIN BERRY *A. brevipedunculata* *A. b.* 'Elegans'	Woody, deciduous vines with beautiful ¹/₄-in. berries in late summer and fall. A. arborea has 2-part leaves and dark blue fruits. A. brevipedunculata has 3-lobed leaves; its turquoise berries turn deep purple. 'Elegans' has variegated foliage.	●	Early to mid-summer	Height: 15–25' Spread: 5–10' Spacing: 3–7'	A. arb. 7 to 9 A. brev. 4 to 8	Full sun to light shade. Ordinary, well-drained soil; tolerant of dry, rocky conditions. In optimal conditions plants can be very invasive. Plant in tubs or in hanging baskets to restrict roots. 'Elegans' is less rampant. Provide support for vines.
ARCTO-STAPHYLOS EMERALD CARPET MANZANITA *Arctostaphylos* 'Emerald Carpet' BEARBERRY *A. uva-ursi*	Mat-forming, woody, evergreen ground covers with oval, 1-in. leaves. Clusters of white, urn-shaped flowers produce bright red, ¹/₃-in. berries. A. uva-ursi has glossy, dark green leaves; those of 'Emerald Carpet' are bright green.	○ ●	Mid-spring	Height: 6–12" Spread: 10–50' Spacing: 2–3'	2 to 7	Full sun to light shade. Well-drained, slightly acid, sandy soil. Both forms tolerate salt spray and winds. Set container-grown plants at 2-ft. intervals. Plants are sensitive to trampling.
ARISTO-LOCHIA DUTCHMAN'S-PIPE, PIPE VINE *Aristolochia durior*	A deciduous, woody perennial vine bearing 6- to 12-in., heart- or kidney-shaped leaves. The tubular, 3-in., ill scented flowers are shaped like tiny pipes, with greenish yellow "stems" and brown "bowls."	● ●	Mid- to late spring	Height: to 30' Spread: 2–5' Spacing: 3–7'	4 to 8	Full sun to full shade. Moist, humus-rich, well-drained soil. Aristolochia grows rapidly and can reach 20 or 30 ft. in a single season. It is excellent as an arbor cover or a screening plant. Provide support for vines.
ASARUM WILD GINGER *Asarum canadense* EUROPEAN WILD GINGER *A. europaeum*	Perennials grown as ground covers with rootstocks that smell and taste like ginger. The heart-shaped leaves arch over to hide 3-part, ¹/₂-in., thimble-shaped maroon flowers. A. canadense is deciduous and A. europaeum is evergreen.	●	Spring	Height: 6–9" Spread: 6–12" Spacing: 6–12"	A. canad. 3 to 7 A. euro. 5 to 9	Partial to full shade. Moist, loamy soil that never completely dries out. Asarum is easy to grow and will spread slowly with time. Creeping rootstocks can be easily divided. Plants are useful in rock gardens.
ASTILBE DWARF CHINESE ASTILBE *Astilbe chinensis* 'Pumila' *A. simplicifolia* 'Sprite'	Perennial ground covers that form low mats of ferny, dark green leaves. 'Pumila' bears clusters of fluffy pink flowers atop erect, 1-ft. stems. 'Sprite' has pink flowers and dark bronze leaves.	●	Mid- to late summer	'Pumila' Height: 8–10" Spread: 6–8" 'Sprite' Height: 8–12" Spread: 1–2'	4 to 8	Partial shade. Moist, loamy soil that never completely dries out. Astilbes are easy to grow and spread slowly with time. Divide plants every several years as they become overcrowded. Space plants 6 to 12 in. apart.

		Flower Color	Time of Bloom	Growth Habit	Hardiness Zones	Growing Conditions
ATHYRIUM JAPANESE PAINTED FERN *Athyrium goeringianum* 'Pictum'	*A deciduous fern with gray-green, 1- to 1½-ft.-long fronds that are tinged with purple at the leaflet bases and then turn lavender and gray toward the tips.*		No flowers	Height: 1–1½' Spread: 6–9" Spacing: 6–8"	3 to 8	*Filtered sun to medium shade. Moist, well-drained, acid, humus-rich soil. Japanese painted fern grows best where the climate is cool and damp. Plants spread slowly with age. Propagate by spores in late summer.*
BACCHARIS DWARF COYOTE BRUSH *Baccharis pilularis*	*A low-growing evergreen shrub native to coastal California. Its branches are covered with bright green, ½- to 1-in.-long, toothed leaves, which overpower small white flowers. Female plants have plumed seeds that may look messy.*	○	Autumn	Height: 1–2' Spread: 5–10' Spacing: 5–7'	7 to 11	*Full sun. Well-drained soil with periodic moisture. Baccharis is an ideal ground cover for southwestern gardens. Prune old growth in late autumn.*
BIGNONIA CROSS VINE *Bignonia capreolata*	*A semideciduous, woody vine native to the Southeast. Each leaf has two 4- to 6-in., lance-shaped leaflets. Clusters of 2-in., trumpet-shaped, red-orange flowers dangle at the ends of short branches and produce narrow, 7-in., podlike fruits.*	● ●	Mid- to late spring	Height: 10–50' Spread: 5–10' Spacing: 5–7'	6 to 9	*Full sun to shade. Well-drained, evenly moist, humus-rich soil. Bignonia climbs rapidly by means of tendrils and is excellent for covering trellises and fences. Prune to keep it an appropriate size.*
BOUGAIN-VILLEA BOUGAINVILLEA *Bougainvillea × buttiana*	*A woody, evergreen perennial vine with 1½- to 3-in., glossy leaves. Flowers are surrounded by 3 vividly colored, papery, petallike bracts. Cultivars offer a wide variety of bract colors, ranging from red to orange to yellow to purple.*	○ ○ ● ● ● ●	Dry season	Height: 5–15' Spread: 2–5' Spacing: 2–4'	10 to 11	*Full sun to very light shade. Well-drained soil; flowers best after dry periods. Prune back lateral growth to 1 in. in spring. Tie vines to supports. Bougainvillea can be grown indoors in pots. Whiteflies and mealybugs may be problems.*
BOUTELOUA SIDEOATS GRAMA *Bouteloua curtipendula* BLUE GRAMA *B. gracilis*	*Delicate-looking native grasses from the East to the Great Plains chiefly valued as fodder for livestock. Pear-like fruits on one side of the stem (B. curtipendula) or in arching combs (B. gracilis) make them handsome garden plants.*	●	B. curt. Late spring B. grac. Late spring to early summer	B. curt. Height: 1–2½' Spread: 1–2' B. grac. Height: 8–24" Spread: 6–12"	B. curt. 4 to 9 B. grac. 3 to 10	*Full sun. Well-drained, fertile soil. These warm-season grasses withstand drought, heat, cold, and even mowing once established. Sow as with grass seed.*

Indicates species shown

Ground Covers & Vines

		Flower Color	Time of Bloom	Growth Habit	Hardiness Zones	Growing Conditions
BUCHLOE BUFFALO GRASS *Buchloe dactyloides*	A sod-forming perennial native to short-grass prairies. It has curly, 1/10-in.-wide, 2-in.-long gray-green leaves and short flower shoots. The foliage turns lavender in autumn and tan in winter. There are separate male and female plants.	●	Late spring to midsummer	Height: 2–8" Spread: 6–12"	3 to 9	Full sun. Well-drained soil; clay loam is best. Once established, buffalo grass is heat and drought tolerant. Plants spread slowly and withstand light foot traffic, forming a good lawn substitute in dry climates. Sow as with grass seed.
CALLIRHOE WINECUP *Callirhoe involucrata*	A sprawling perennial native to the Great Plains. It produces abundant, chalice-shaped, 1- to 2-in., hollyhock like flowers. Each wine red petal has a white splotch at its base. The hairy, dark green leaves have 5–7 lobes.	● ●	Early spring to early summer	Height: 6–36" Spread: 1–3' Spacing: 1–2'	4 to 8	Full sun. Well-drained, slightly acid soil. Plants are drought resistant. Prolong the flowering season by removing flowers as they fade. Callirhoe is excellent for rock gardens, on sunny banks, and as a ground cover.
CALLUNA SCOTCH HEATHER *Calluna vulgaris*	A small, mat-forming, evergreen shrub whose dense branches bear tiny (1/8-in.) leaves. Small rosy lavender flowers are borne on 1- to 10-in.-long racemes and attract bees.	● ●	Midsummer to early autumn	Height: 6–24" Spread: 2–8' Spacing: 2–3'	4 to 6	Full sun. Evenly moist, well-drained, humus-rich, acid (pH 6 or less) soil of low fertility. Do not fertilize or add lime. Prune in early spring. Japanese beetles can be a problem. Scotch heather is a superb ground cover or rock garden plant.
CAMPSIS TRUMPET CREEPER *Campsis radicans*	A deciduous, woody native vine with 3-in., tubular, 5-lobed, bright red-orange (or yellow) tubular flowers and glossy green compound leaves with 7–11 leaflets. Vines climb by aerial rootlets.	● ● ●	Midsummer to early autumn	Height: 10–40' Spread: 1–2' Spacing: 1–2'	4 to 9	Full sun to light shade. Fertile, moist soil. Plants need protection from winter winds in zone 5 and colder. Campsis benefits from annual pruning in early spring. Vines may require support.
CARPOBROTUS HOTTENTOT FIG, ICE PLANT *Carpobrotus edulis*	A mat-forming, succulent perennial ground cover. Its 4- to 5-in., fleshy leaves are triangular in cross section. The 2- to 3-in. flowers have many thin yellow, yellow-pink, or purple petals around masses of yellow stamens. Figlike fruits are not tasty.	● ● ●	Spring to summer	Height: 5–6" Spread: 1–50' Spacing: 1–3'	10 to 11	Full sun. Well-drained soil. Plants are quite drought tolerant and resistant to salt spray once established. Carpobrotus does well in coastal gardens.

		Flower Color	Time of Bloom	Growth Habit	Hardiness Zones	Growing Conditions
	CEANOTHUS POINT RÉYES CEANOTHUS *Ceanothus gloriosus* 'Anchor Bay' CARMEL CREEPER ◄ *C. griseus* var. *horizontalis*	● ●	Early to mid-spring	C. glor. Height: 1½–2½' Spread: 6–8' C. gris. Height: 1½–2½' Spread: 5–15'	8 to 9	Full sun. Well-drained, rocky soil. Plants are prone to root rot if soil is too moist and are quite drought resistant, especially during the summer. Ceanothus grows best in Pacific Coast gardens and makes a good ground cover. Space plants 4 to 8 ft. apart.
	CELASTRUS AMERICAN BITTER-SWEET *Celastrus scandens*		Spring	Height: 10–25' Spread: 4–6' Spacing: 3–4'	3 to 8	Full sun to light shade. Any kind of soil. In fertile soil this vine can become rampant, sometimes killing trees it climbs upon. Grow both male and female plants to ensure fruit production.
	CERASTIUM SNOW-IN-SUMMER *Cerastium tomentosum*	○	Early to mid-summer	Height: 4–10" Spread: 6–12" Spacing: 6–12"	2 to 7	Full sun. Well-drained, sandy loam. Plants may rot in wet soil. Cerastium is excellent for rock gardens and steep banks but spreads rapidly and may overrun other, more delicate plants.
	CERATO-STIGMA LEADWORT *Ceratostigma plumbaginoides*	●	Midsummer to mid-autumn	Height: 1–1½' Spread: 1–1½' Spacing: 9–15"	5 to 9	Full sun to light shade. Well-drained soil of average fertility; Ceratostigma does not grow well if soil is too moist. Mulch plants during winter in zones 5–7.
	CHAMAE-MELUM ROMAN CHAMOMILE ◄ *Chamaemelum nobile* *C. nobile* 'Treneague'	○	Late spring to late summer	Height: 6–12" Spread: 6–12" Spacing: 6–12"	3 to 10	Full sun to partial shade. Well-drained, sandy soil. Sow the fine seeds on the soil surface, and keep moist until seedlings are established. Harvest flower heads as outer petals start to curve back.

◄ *Indicates species shown*

Ground Covers & Vines

		Flower Color	Time of Bloom	Growth Habit	Hardiness Zones	Growing Conditions
	CHRYSO-GONUM GREEN-AND-GOLD, GOLDEN STAR *Chrysogonum virginianum*	A long-blooming native perennial used as a ground cover or bedding plant. It bears single, bright gold, daisylike flowers with pointed petals. Flowers are borne on short stems above a spreading, dense mat of lustrous green leaves.	○	Early spring to midsummer	Height: 6–12" Spread: 6–12" Spacing: 6–9"	4 to 9	Full sun to medium shade, with some afternoon shade in warm climates. Well-drained, moist soil. Mulch very lightly during winter in cooler climates. Remove mulch early in spring; plants may rot if mulch is too thick.
	CISTUS ROCK ROSE *Cistus salviifolius*	A spreading evergreen shrub bearing gray-green, 1-in. leaves with a crinkled texture. White, 1½- to 2-in. flowers, with yellow blotches at their centers, are short-lived, but a long flowering season ensures a profusion of bloom.	○	Late spring to early summer	Height: 1–3' Spread: 2–6' Spacing: 2–4'	9 to 11	Full sun to light shade. Well-drained, alkaline, sandy soil. Rock rose is an excellent ground cover for warm, sunny banks in frost-free regions.
	CLEMATIS EVERGREEN CLEMATIS *Clematis armandii*	A genus of fast-growing, woody or semiwoody, climbing vines with showy, flat, round flowers that produce attractive fuzzy fruits. Evergreen C. armandii has 3- to 5-in., narrow leaves and fragrant, 2- to 2½-in. white flowers.	○	Spring	Height: 10–15' Spread: 1–2' Spacing: 1–2'	7 to 9	Partial sun to partial shade. Evenly moist, well-drained soil. Mulch to provide a cool root environment in summer. Prune in summer after flowering is finished and seeds are shed. Provide support for vines.
	CLEMATIS FLORIDA CLEMATIS *Clematis florida*	A deciduous vine with shiny, smooth, deep green leaves that are hairy beneath. The 3-in. flowers have purple stamens surrounded by 2 large creamy white bracts and 4–8 green-striped petal-like sepals.	○	Summer	Height: 6–12' Spread: 1–2' Spacing: 1–2'	6 to 9	Partial sun to partial shade. Evenly moist, well-drained soil. Mulch to provide a cool root environment in summer. Prune only lightly in late winter. Provide support for vines.
	CLEMATIS JACKMAN CLEMATIS *Clematis × jackmanii*	A deciduous vine with large (4- to 7-in.), showy flowers that are usually purple-blue, but may be blue, red, or violet, depending on the cultivar. The attractive fruits are covered with long, silky hairs.	●●●	Late spring to frost	Height: 8–18' Spread: 1–2' Spacing: 1–2'	3 to 8	Partial sun to partial shade. Evenly moist, well-drained soil. Mulch to provide a cool root environment in summer. Prune in early spring, before vines start growing. Provide support for vines.

			Flower Color	Time of Bloom	Growth Habit	Hardiness Zones	Growing Conditions
	CLEMATIS ANEMONE CLEMATIS *Clematis montana* 'Alba'	A vigorously growing deciduous vine that quickly covers arbors or walls. The 2- to 3½-in. white flowers each have 4 sepals and are borne in clusters of 1–5 on long (2- to 5-in.) stems.	○	Late spring to summer	Height: 10–25' Spread: 2–4' Spacing: 1–3'	5 to 9	Partial sun to partial shade. Evenly moist, well-drained soil. Mulch to provide a cool root environment in summer. Prune in summer after flowering is finished and seeds are shed. Provide support for vines.
	CLEMATIS SWEET AUTUMN CLEMATIS *Clematis paniculata* (*C. maximowicziana*)	A deciduous vine with many small (1- to 1½-in.) flowers borne in showy clusters in late summer. Fluffy, attractive fruits follow in autumn. Leathery leaves have egg-shaped leaflets.	○	Late summer to autumn	Height: 10–30' Spread: 5–10' Spacing: 2–5'	5 to 9	Partial sun to partial shade; one of the most shade-tolerant clematises. Evenly moist, well-drained soil. Mulch to provide a cool root environment in summer. Provide support for vines. Prune in early spring, before vines start growing.
	CLEMATIS GOLDEN CLEMATIS ◄ *Clematis tangutica* SCARLET CLEMATIS *C. texensis*	Climbing, deciduous vines with solitary, nodding, bell-shaped flowers from midsummer until the first frost. C. tangutica has 3- to 4-in. bright yellow flowers; those of C. texensis are ½ to 1 in. long and range in color from rosy pink to bright red.	◑ ●	Midsummer to autumn	Height: 5–10' Spread: 2–6' Spacing: 2–4'	5 to 9	Partial sun to partial shade. Evenly moist, well-drained soil. Mulch to provide a cool root environment in summer. Provide support for vines. Prune in early spring, before vines start growing.
	COBAEA CUP-AND-SAUCER VINE *Cobaea scandens*	A fast-growing vine that climbs by tendrils. Showy, 1- to 2½-in., violet-and-white cuplike flowers are surrounded by saucerlike green calyxes. Golden stamens protrude from flower centers. A white-flowered form is available.	○ ●	Late spring to frost	Height: 10–25' Spread: 1–2' Spacing: 1–2'	9 to 11 (Grow as a tender annual in colder regions)	Full sun. Well-drained, sandy soil of low or average fertility. Cobaea does best if provided with support.
	CONVALLARIA LILY-OF-THE-VALLEY *Convallaria majalis*	A hardy perennial that forms a dense ground cover with attractive, spear-shaped, deep green leaves. One-sided sprays of fragrant, nodding, ¼-in., bell-shaped white flowers appear in late spring.	○	Late spring	Height: 6–12" Spread: 4–8" Spacing: 4–8"	3 to 8	Partial to full shade. Moist, well-drained soil rich in organic matter. With age, lily-of-the-valley forms mats that should be divided and replanted to maintain vigorous growth and flowering.

◄ Indicates species shown

Ground Covers & Vines

			Flower Color	Time of Bloom	Growth Habit	Hardiness Zones	Growing Conditions
	CORNUS BUNCHBERRY *Cornus canadensis*	A flowering dogwood relative that sprawls along the ground. The 1- to 3-in. leaves are attached in whorls to semiwoody stems. Small, greenish white flowers, each surrounded by 4 white bracts, produce bright red, $^1/_4$-in. berries.	○	Late spring	Height: 4–9" Spread: 6–24" Spacing: 6–12"	2 to 6	Filtered sun to moderate shade. Moist, acid, peaty soil. In full sun the leaves are small and stunted. Bunchberry doesn't grow well where summers are hot or dry.
	COTONEASTER CREEPING COTONEASTER *Cotoneaster adpressus* CRANBERRY COTONEASTER ◀ *C. apiculatus*	Low-growing, spreading deciduous shrubs bearing beautiful pink $^1/_4$-in. flowers that produce bright red, $^1/_4$-in. berries by late summer. C. adpressus has a lower, more spreading form. C. apiculatus has reddish stems with sharply angled twigs.	●	Mid- to late spring	C. adpr. Height: 1–1$^1/_2$' Spread: 4–6' C. apic. Height: 2–3' Spread: 3–6'	4 to 7	Full sun to partial shade. Well-drained, moist, humus-rich soil. Once established, both species tolerate dry soil and windy conditions. Plants spread horizontally with age. Space plants 2 to 4 ft. apart.
	COTONEASTER BEARBERRY COTONEASTER *Cotoneaster dammeri*	A low-growing, spreading deciduous shrub with small ($^3/_4$- to 1-in.), glossy, elliptical, semievergreen leaves borne on thin branches. Where winters are mild, leaves persist until spring. Flowers are white or pink and $^1/_3$ to $^1/_2$ in. long.	○ ●	Late spring	Height: 1–2' Spread: 3–6' Spacing: 2–4'	5 to 8	Full sun to partial shade. Well-drained, evenly moist, acid, humus-rich soil. Once established, bearberry cotoneaster tolerates dry soil and windy conditions. Plants spread horizontally with age.
	COTONEASTER ROCKSPRAY COTONEASTER *Cotoneaster horizontalis*	A low-growing deciduous shrub with tiny ($^1/_5$- to $^1/_2$-in.) leaves outlining the horizontal sprays of branches, which resemble fish backbones. Pink flowers, only $^1/_4$ in. wide, are massed in great numbers. This spreading shrub can climb walls.	●	Late spring	Height: 2–3' Spread: 5–8' Spacing: 3–6'	4 to 8	Full sun to partial shade. Well-drained, moist, humus-rich soil. Once established, rockspray cotoneaster tolerates dry soil and windy conditions. Plants spread horizontally with age.
	CUCURBITA YELLOW-FLOWERED GOURD *Cucurbita pepo* var. *ovifera*	An annual vine with hairy stems and large, triangular leaves. Yellow, 5-petaled flowers produce hard-shelled, egg-shaped or crook-necked, 3- to 6-in. fruits in a variety of colors, textures, and patterns.	●	Summer	Vine Height: 8–15' Spread: 5–15' Ground cover Height: 1–2' Spacing: 1–2'	Tender annual	Full sun. Well-drained, sandy loam of average to low fertility. Sow seeds $^1/_2$ in. deep in late spring after all danger of frost has passed. Provide support for vines, or let them sprawl along the ground.

			Flower Color	Time of Bloom	Growth Habit	Hardiness Zones	Growing Conditions
	DENNSTAEDTIA HAY-SCENTED FERN *Dennstaedtia punctilobula*	A deciduous, creeping fern native to the eastern U.S. Soft, fuzzy, 1- to 2-ft. leaves smell like freshly mowed hay if crushed. The fronds are divided into about 20 pairs of leaflets, each of which is further subdivided, giving a lacy appearance.		No flowers	Height: 9–16" Spread: 6–9" Spacing: 6–8"	3 to 8	Full sun to light shade. Humus-rich soil. Hay-scented fern grows well in woodland gaps and on rocky sites. Plants spread rapidly from rootstocks and are difficult to eradicate once established.
	DOLICHOS HYACINTH BEAN *Dolichos lablab*	A semiwoody vine bearing attractive purplish leaves, each with 3 leaflets, and 3/4- to 1-in., pink, purple, or white pealike flowers. Flowers produce showy, flat, 1- to 3-in., bright magenta or purple edible pods.	○◍●	Summer	Height: 10–30' Spread: 3–6' Spacing: 2–3'	10 to 11 (Grow as a half-hardy annual in colder regions)	Full sun. Average, well-drained, fertile soil. In zone 9 and colder, sow seeds 1 in. deep after the last spring frost.
	EPIMEDIUM RED ALPINE EPIMEDIUM *Epimedium alpinum* var. *rubrum* BISHOP'S HAT ◀ *E. grandiflorum*	Durable perennial ground covers with ornate flowers and leaves divided into 6–9 heart-shaped leaflets. The 1- to 2-in. flowers of E. grandiflorum are red, white, or violet; E. alpinum var. rubrum has smaller red-and-yellow flowers.	○◍●●	Late spring	Height: 8–12" Spread: 6–12" Spacing: 6–12"	5 to 9	Partial to full shade. Well-drained, humus-rich soil. Once established, Epimedium will tolerate dry conditions. Cut off old foliage in late winter before new leaves sprout.
	ERICA SNOW HEATHER, SPRING HEATH *Erica carnea*	A low evergreen shrub closely related to Scotch heather (Calluna). This species complements autumn-blooming heather by producing its bell-shaped, rosy flowers earlier. The tiny leaves are in whorls of 4.	○◍●	Late winter to early spring	Height: 4–8" Spread: 2–4' Spacing: 1–3'	5 to 7	Full sun. Evenly moist, well-drained, humus-rich, acid (pH 6 or less) soil of low fertility. Acid soil is essential for its growth; do not fertilize or add lime. Requires the same conditions as Scotch heather (Calluna).
	EUONYMUS WINTERCREEPER *Euonymus fortunei*	A highly variable species of woody evergreen. Both vine and shrub forms are available. Its 3/4- to 1-in., oblong leaves are typically dark green with yellow or white veins or variegations. Vine forms are used as ground covers or climbers.	◍	Early summer	Vine Height: 4–8' Spread: 10–20' Ground cover Height: 3–6' Spacing: 2–3'	5 to 9	Full sun to shade. Well-drained, ordinary garden soil. Euonymus is tolerant of almost any soil but will not survive poor drainage. Plants are susceptible to attack by euonymus scale insects.

◀ *Indicates species shown*

Ground Covers & Vines

		Flower Color	Time of Bloom	Growth Habit	Hardiness Zones	Growing Conditions
FESTUCA BLUE FESCUE, SHEEP'S FESCUE *Festuca ovina var. glauca*	*A low, tufted grass with silvery blue-green, wiry leaves. Short panicles of flowers grow above the clumps of soft foliage. Blue fescue makes an attractive edging plant but does not withstand foot traffic.*	● ○	*Spring to early summer*	Height: 4–18" Spread: 6–8" Spacing: 4–8"	4 to 9	*Full sun to partial shade. Prefers moist, well-drained soil but will tolerate some drought if temperatures are not too high. Plant in partial shade and provide extra water in hot regions. Cut back tops in autumn.*
FICUS CLIMBING FIG *Ficus pumila*	*An evergreen vine that attaches to surfaces by roots as it climbs. Young leaves are heart-shaped but become 2- to 4-in. ovals in maturity. The pear-shaped fruits are 2 in. long.*	●	*Inconspicuous flowers*	Height: 1–2' Spread: 10–20' Spacing: 2–5'	9 to 11	*Partial sun to full shade. Moist, humus-rich, well-drained soil. Climbing fig grows best on north- and east-facing surfaces out of direct sun. Cut back to the ground if necessary to discourage rampant growth.*
FRAGARIA BEACH STRAWBERRY *Fragaria chiloensis* WILD STRAWBERRY ◀ *F. virginiana*	*Perennial ground covers with compound leaves that have 3 toothed leaflets. The 1/2-in., roselike flowers have white petals and golden centers. F. chiloensis has 1-in. berries; those of F. virginiana are smaller but very flavorful.*	○	*Mid- to late spring*	Height: 3–6" Spread: 3–6" Spacing: 1–2'	3 to 7	*Full sun to partial shade. Well-drained, acid, evenly moist, humus-rich soil. These strawberry species spread rapidly.*
GALAX COLTSFOOT *Galax urceolata* *(G. aphylla)*	*An evergreen perennial native to the woods of the southern Appalachians. Long spikes of tiny white flowers are borne above lustrous, rounded, 5-in.-wide leaves that turn bronze in autumn.*	○	*Early to mid-summer*	Height: 1–1½' Spread: 6–18" Spacing: 6–18"	6 to 8	*Filtered sun to full shade. Evenly moist, well-drained, humus-rich, acid soil. Galax spreads slowly with age and makes an ideal ground cover.*
GALIUM SWEET WOODRUFF *Galium odoratum*	*An easy-to-grow perennial ground cover with 1- to 2-in. leaves arranged in whorls of 6–8 around square stems. The cross-shaped, 1/3-in. white flowers are borne in loose clusters above the foliage. All parts of the plant are fragrant.*	○	*Spring*	Height: 8–12" Spread: 6–12" Spacing: 6–12"	4 to 8	*Partial shade. Well-drained, evenly moist soil. Sweet woodruff may spread rapidly and become weedy in sites with abundant organic matter and moisture.*

			Flower Color	Time of Bloom	Growth Habit	Hardiness Zones	Growing Conditions
	GAULTHERIA TEABERRY, WINTERGREEN *Gaultheria procumbens*	*A low-growing evergreen plant with ½-in., urn-shaped, pendent white flowers producing red, ¼-in. berries that last into winter. The wintergreen-flavored leaves are bright green when young but become leathery and reddish in fall.*	○	*Early to mid-summer*	Height: 2–4" Spread: 4–12" Spacing: 3–6"	3 to 8	*Filtered sun to full shade, but grows best in sunny patches. Dry or wet, acid, humus-rich soil. Wintergreen makes a good ground cover.*
	GAULTHERIA SALAL *Gaultheria shallon*	*A woody, evergreen shrub native to the Pacific Coast. Urn-shaped, pink or white, ½-in.-long flowers dangle in 6-in. clusters and produce dark purple fruits that turn black with age. The 2- to 4-in. leaves are round, glossy, and leathery.*	●	*Mid-spring to early summer*	Height: 2–8' Spread: 2–6' Spacing: 2–4'	5 to 9	*Full sun to light shade, but grows best in sunny patches. Dry or wet, acid, humus-rich soil.*
	GELSEMIUM CAROLINA YELLOW JESSAMINE, YELLOW TRUMPET FLOWER *Gelsemium sempervirens*	*A woody, twining, evergreen vine native to the Southeast. It has pairs of 4-in., lance-shaped leaves on thin, wiry stems. The bell-shaped, fragrant, 1- to 1½-in., 5-lobed flowers are yellow.*	●	*Late winter to early spring, sometimes in autumn*	Vine Height: 10–20' Spread: 3–4' Ground cover Height: 1–2' Spacing: 1–3'	6 to 9	*Full sun to medium shade. Moist, well-drained, humus-rich soil. Gelsemium looks most attractive when grown over supports such as fences or trellises. It is also used as a ground cover on banks.*
	GERANIUM HARDY GERANIUM *Geranium dalmaticum* LANCASTER GERANIUM ◀ *G. sanguineum* var. *lancastrense*	*Mound-forming perennials with 5-lobed, deeply dissected, dark green leaves. G. dalmaticum has leaves that turn yellow and red in fall and light pink flowers. G. sanguineum var. lancastrense has showy, 5-petaled pink flowers with darker veins.*	●	*Summer*	G. dalm. Height: 3–4" Spread: 6–12" G. sang. Height: 4–8" Spread: 1–1½'	4 to 8	*Full sun to partial shade, with some afternoon shade in warm climates. Well-drained, moist soil that is rich in organic matter. Both types spread slowly with time. Space plants 6 to 12 in. apart.*
	HEDERA ALGERIAN IVY, CANARY IVY *Hedera canariensis*	*A woody, evergreen vine that climbs by aerial roots. It bears oval or triangular, 5- to 8-in. leaves with shallow lobes. Cultivars vary in leaf size and variegation. H. canariensis can be grown as a ground cover.*	●	*Late summer to mid-autumn*	Vine Height: 10–20' Spread: 10–15' Ground cover Height: 6–18" Spacing: 4–8'	9 to 11	*Partial sun to partial shade. Moist, humus-rich soil. Avoid hot, dry locations in full sun; these conditions cause leaves to turn brown. Slugs and snails may be problems.*

◀ *Indicates species shown*

Ground Covers & Vines

		Flower Color	Time of Bloom	Growth Habit	Hardiness Zones	Growing Conditions
HEDERA ENGLISH IVY *Hedera helix*	An evergreen perennial vine with dark green, leathery, roughly triangular leaves. The many cultivars vary in leaf lobes, variegation, and hardiness. Grow ivy as a houseplant, ground cover, or clinging climber.	●	Mid-autumn	Vine Height: 3"–30' Spread: 1–15' Ground cover Height: 6–18" Spacing: 1–2'	4 to 9	Full sun to full shade, with some afternoon shade in warm climates. Moist, well-drained, humus-rich soil. English ivy is not particular about soil acidity. Select hardy cultivars, such as 'Bulgaria', for cold regions.
HEMERO-CALLIS CITRON DAYLILY ◀ *Hemerocallis citrina* TAWNY DAYLILY *H. fulva*	Perennials with large, trumpet-shaped flowers that last only a day. Numerous buds give these plants a long blooming season. H. citrina has fragrant, 6-in., light yellow flowers. H. fulva has 3- to 4-in., tawny orange flowers.	○ ●	Late spring to summer	Height: 1–5' Spread: 1½–2' Spacing: 1–2'	3 to 9	Full sun to light shade; shade in warm climates. Humus-rich, evenly moist soil. Divide plants periodically to keep flowering vigorous. Root-stocks spread with age. These species spread more quickly than hybrid daylilies.
HEMERO-CALLIS HYBRID DAYLILY *Hemerocallis hybrids* ◀ *H. 'Stella d'Oro'*	Perennials with mounds of grasslike leaves and large (up to 7-in.) flowers in an array of colors from white to yellow to dark red. Flower color patterns range from uniform to bicolored to banded; forms range from trumpets to stars to doubles.	○ ○ ● ● ●	Early spring to summer, depending on cultivar	Height: 1–5' Spread: 1–1½' Spacing: 1–2'	3 to 9	Full sun to light shade; shade in warm climates. Humus-rich, evenly moist soil. Divide plants periodically to keep flowering vigorous. The rootstocks spread slowly with age.
HOSTA NARROW-LEAVED PLANTAIN LILY *Hosta lancifolia*	A slow-growing perennial grown as a ground cover or bedding plant. Violet, 1½- to 2-in.-long flowers are borne on shoots above clumps of glossy, dark green, narrow, 6-in. leaves.	●	Late summer to autumn	Height: 1½–2' Spread: 1–1½' Spacing: 9–12"	4 to 8	Partial sun to full shade. Evenly moist, well-drained, humus-rich soil. Sufficient moisture is essential, but hostas are prone to rot if soil is soggy. Mulch during winter in cold regions. Slugs and deer may be problems.
HOSTA FRANCES WILLIAMS HOSTA *Hosta sieboldiana* 'Frances Williams'	A perennial ground cover with rounded, puckered, 10-in.-long blue-green leaves variegated with yellow. Pale lavender, 1- to 1½-in. flowers are borne in clusters above the foliage. Mass plantings of this hosta make a good tall ground cover.	●	Midsummer	Height: 2–2½' Spread: 3–3½' Spacing: 1½–2½'	4 to 8	Partial sun to full shade. Evenly moist, well-drained, humus-rich soil. Sufficient moisture is essential, but hostas are prone to rot if soil is soggy. Mulch during winter in cold regions. Slugs and deer may be problems.

		Flower Color	Time of Bloom	Growth Habit	Hardiness Zones	Growing Conditions
HOUTTUYNIA CHAMELEON PLANT *Houttuynia cordata* 'Chameleon'	A perennial ground cover that forms mounds of 2- to 3-in., aromatic, heart-shaped leaves variegated with green, yellow, and red. The ¹/₂- to 2-in.-long, cylindrical spikes of tiny white flowers are surrounded by 4 white, petallike bracts.	○	Early summer	Height: 6–9" Spread: 1–2' Spacing: 1–2'	5 to 9	Full sun to partial shade. Moist to wet, humus-rich soil. Houttuynia *spreads rapidly by creeping root-stocks; it can become rampant under ideal conditions. Plant in containers if space is limited.*
HUMULUS COMMON HOP *Humulus lupulus*	A deciduous perennial vine that climbs by twining its stems around supports. Attractive, grapelike, rough-surfaced leaves have 3–5 deep lobes and long stems. Dangling clusters of flowers produce saclike fruits arranged in cones.	●	Summer	Height: 10–25' Spread: 12–18' Spacing: 2–4'	3 to 11	Full sun. Deep, well-drained soil rich in humus. Plant seeds where desired in mid-spring, providing support for vines to twine around. Plants may self-sow or become weedy over the years. Downy mildew can be a problem.
HYDRANGEA CLIMBING HYDRANGEA *Hydrangea anomala* subsp. *petiolaris*	A slow-growing, deciduous, woody vine with attractive, peeling, cinnamon-brown bark and pairs of glossy, dark green, broad, oval 2- to 4-in. leaves. Small white flowers with outer rings of larger (1- to 2-in.) florets form 6- to 10-in. clusters.	○	Late spring to early summer	Height: 10–80' Spread: 12–18' Spacing: 6–10'	5 to 7	Full sun to shade. Humus-rich, fertile, moist, well-drained soil. Climbing hydrangea will go up trees, fences, brick walls, and other structures.
HYPERICUM AARON'S-BEARD, CREEPING ST.-JOHN'S-WORT *Hypericum calycinum*	A low-growing semiever-green shrub with pairs of oval leaves with veiny undersides and showy, yellow, 2- to 3-in. flowers.	○	Early summer to early autumn	Height: 1–1¹/₂' Spread: 1–2' Spacing: 1–2'	6 to 9	Full sun to partial shade. Not choosy about soil conditions. Prune in late winter to remove deadwood and stimulate vigorous growth and flowering.
IPOMOEA MOONFLOWER *Ipomoea alba*	A climbing vine with heart-shaped leaves, somewhat prickly stems, and milky sap. The fragrant, 5-lobed, 6-in.-wide, cup-shaped, white flowers open at night.	○	Summer	Height: 6–10' Spread: 1–1¹/₂' Spacing: 8–12"	10 to 11 (Grow as a tender annual in colder regions)	Full sun. Average to moist, well-drained soil that is not too rich in organic matter. Soak seeds overnight before planting. Sow seeds where plants are desired after all danger of frost has passed. Provide support for vines.

◄ *Indicates species shown*

Ground Covers & Vines

		Flower Color	Time of Bloom	Growth Habit	Hardiness Zones	Growing Conditions
IPOMOEA SCARLET STAR-GLORY *Ipomoea coccinea* CARDINAL CLIMBER ◄ *I. × multifida*	Annual vines with red flowers. I. coccinea has heart-shaped, 6-in. leaves and 1- to 1½-in., yellow-throated flowers. I. × multifida has broad, feathery leaves cut into segments and 2-in., white-throated flowers.	●	Summer	Height: 6–10' Spread: 1–1½' Spacing: 8–12"	Tender annual	Full sun. Somewhat dry to moist, well-drained soil that is not too rich in humus. Soak seeds overnight before planting. Sow seeds where plants are desired after danger of frost has passed. Provide support for vines.
IPOMOEA CYPRESS VINE *Ipomoea quamoclit*	An annual vine with slender, 1- to 1½-in.-long, orange or scarlet flowers. The oval leaves are deeply cut into threadlike segments. I. quamoclit is one of the latest-blooming morning glories.	● ●	Summer to early autumn	Height: 10–15' Spread: 1½–2' Spacing: 1–2'	Tender annual	Full sun. Somewhat dry to moist, well-drained soil that is not too rich in humus. Soak seeds overnight before planting. Sow seeds where plants are desired after danger of frost has passed. Provide support for vines.
IPOMOEA MORNING-GLORY *Ipomoea tricolor*	A classic annual vine with large (10-in.), heart-shaped leaves. Flowers are usually sky blue and up to 4 in. wide with white centers. Many cultivars are available with striped petals or different petal colors.	○ ◐ ●	Summer	Height: 6–10' Spread: 1–1½' Spacing: 1–2'	10 to 11 (Grow as a tender annual in colder regions)	Full sun. Somewhat dry to moist, well-drained soil that is not too rich in humus. Soak seeds overnight before planting. Sow seeds where plants are desired after danger of frost has passed. Provide support for vines.
IRIS DWARF CRESTED IRIS *Iris cristata*	A small perennial native to open woodlands. Its 2- to 3-in. flowers possess an elegance often lacking in the showier garden irises. The single blue, purple, or white flowers appear on erect, slender stems amid flat, long leaves.	○ ◐ ●	Mid- to late spring	Height: 3–8" Spread: 2–6' Spacing: 1–2'	5 to 8	Filtered sun to partial shade. Well-drained, evenly moist, humus-rich soil. Irises spread quickly by shallow rhizomes.
JASMINUM SPANISH JASMINE *Jasminum grandiflorum* POET'S JESSAMINE ◄ *J. officinale*	Climbing vines with pairs of leaves with 3–7 leaflets and clusters of fragrant white flowers. J. grandiflorum is evergreen and has up to 50 flowers per cluster. J. officinale is deciduous or semievergreen with about a dozen flowers per cluster.	○	Summer to autumn	Height: 6–40' Spread: 2–6' Spacing: 1–3'	J. grand. 10 to 11 J. offic. 8 to 10	Full sun to partial shade. Evenly moist, well-drained soil of moderate fertility. Both species flower best in full sun. Jasmines are vigorous growers. They attain their greatest height when trained on walls or trellises.

		Flower Color	Time of Bloom	Growth Habit	Hardiness Zones	Growing Conditions
JUNIPERUS SHORE JUNIPER *Juniperus conferta*	An evergreen, matlike, coniferous shrub native to coastal dunes of Japan. Bright blue-green, $1/3$-in., awl-shaped needles are densely clustered in whorls of 3. Berrylike, $1/3$-in. cones are blue-black and covered with a waxy bloom.		Spring	Height: $1–1\frac{1}{2}'$ Spread: 5–10' Spacing: 2–3'	6 to 8	Full sun. Ordinary, well-drained garden soil; does not grow well if soil is poorly drained or clayey. Plants tolerate salt spray. Shore juniper spreads slowly and makes a good ground cover for dry sites.
JUNIPERUS CREEPING JUNIPER *Juniperus horizontalis* ◄ *J. horizontalis* 'Wittonii'	A low, creeping shrub that forms a mat. Dense, spiny or scaly, light blue-green leaves mostly cover the long, trailing branches. Plants bear $1/4$-in., waxy, blue, berrylike cones. 'Bar Harbor', 'Blue Rug', and 'Wiltonii' are popular cultivars.		Spring	Height: 6–24" Spread: 2–6' Spacing: 1–3'	3 to 9	Full sun. Ordinary, well-drained garden soil. Creeping juniper tolerates hot, dry conditions and heavy or rocky soil. It is susceptible to juniper blight but is a useful ground cover for difficult sites.
LAGENARIA CALABASH GOURD, WHITE-FLOWERED GOURD *Lagenaria siceraria*	An annual vine with hairy stems and large heart-shaped leaves. White, 5-petaled flowers produce hard-shelled fruits ranging from 3 to 30 in. in length. Shapes range from spheres to dumbbells.	○	Summer	Vine Height: 8–30' Spread: 5–15' Ground cover Height: 1–2' Spacing: 3–4'	Tender annual	Full sun. Well-drained, sandy loam of average to low fertility. Sow seeds $1/2$ in. deep in late spring after danger of frost has passed. Provide support for vines, or let them sprawl on the ground.
LAMIASTRUM YELLOW ARCHANGEL *Lamiastrum galeobdolon* ◄ *L. galeobdolon* 'Variegatum'	A spreading perennial ground cover with pairs of toothed, oval, 3-in., semievergreen leaves on square stems. Bright yellow, 2-lipped, $1/2$- to 1-in. flowers are borne singly at the bases of leaves and in clusters at the tops of stems.	○	Late spring to early summer	Height: 1–2' Spread: 1–3' Spacing: 1–2'	5 to 9	Full sun to full shade. Well-drained soil. Lamiastrum is easy to grow and can be invasive under conditions of ample moisture and fertile soil.
LAMIUM SPOTTED DEAD NETTLE *Lamium maculatum*	A creeping perennial with 1- to 2-in., lustrous, attractively variegated leaves and clusters of rosy pink or lavender, 1- to 2-in., double-lipped flowers. Cultivars with white flowers and different leaf variegations are available.	○ ● ●	Late spring to summer	Height: 6–12" Spread: 6–8" Spacing: 4–6"	4 to 9	Dappled sun to full shade. Moist, well-drained, acid soil. Spotted dead nettle spreads with time; it makes an attractive ground cover but can be invasive.

◄ *Indicates species shown*

Ground Covers & Vines

		Flower Color	Time of Bloom	Growth Habit	Hardiness Zones	Growing Conditions
LANTANA TRAILING LANTANA *Lantana montevidensis*	A vinelike shrub with soft, trailing stems bearing pairs of 1-in., toothed leaves with a crinkled surface. The 1½-in.-wide clusters of small, tubular, rosy lilac flowers produce blackberry-like fruits. Both fruits and foliage are poisonous.	●●	Summer, or year-round in warm climates	Height: 2–4' Spread: 2–6' Spacing: 1–3'	9 to 11 (Grow as a half-hardy annual in colder regions)	Full sun. Well-drained soil of average fertility. Lantana *is prone to mildew and rot in moist soil and in shade. It is useful as a potted plant or ground cover.*
LATHYRUS EVERLASTING PEA *Lathyrus grandiflorus* PERENNIAL PEA ◄ *L. latifolius*	Perennial vines with 1- to 2-in., showy flowers. L. grandi-florus has clusters of 2 to 3 fragrant magenta flowers. L. latifolius has several rose-red, pink, yellow, blue, or white flowers per cluster.		Summer to early autumn	Height: 4–8' Spread: 1–3' Spacing: 6–12"	4 to 9	Full sun. Well-drained, evenly moist soil. Lathyrus *is prone to rot if soil is too soggy. Provide support for vines. Remove old flowers to prolong flowering. Both species make good covers for fences and trellises.*
LATHYRUS SWEET PEA *Lathyrus odoratus*	A hardy annual vine bearing clusters of fragrant, 1- to 2-in. flowers in white, pink, red, or purple. Fruits are 2-in.-long, hairy pods. Cultivars include bush and dwarf forms.	○●●●	Late spring to midsummer	Height: 4–6' Spread: 6–15" Spacing: 6–12"	Hardy annual	Full sun. Moist, well-drained, slightly alkaline soil, with additional lime if soil is too acid. In late autumn or early spring, sow seeds 2 in. deep where plants are desired. Provide support for vines. Remove old flowers to prolong flowering.
LIRIOPE BIG BLUE LILYTURF *Liriope muscari* CREEPING LILYTURF ◄ *L. spicata*	Grasslike perennial members of the lily family that form mounds of blue-green, ¼- to ½-in.-wide, 1- to 2-ft.-long leaves. Dense spikes of hyacinth-like flowers rise above the foliage in summer, followed by pea-size blue fruits.	○●●●	Midsummer	*L. musc.* Height: 8–18" Spread: 1–2' *L. spic.* Height: 5–10" Spread: 1–2'	5 to 10	Full sun to light shade. Evenly moist, well-drained soil. Once established, both species grow well in dry soil. Cut old leaves back in early spring. Space plants 8 to 16 in. apart.
LONICERA EVERBLOOMING HONEYSUCKLE, GOLDFLAME HONEYSUCKLE *Lonicera × heckrottii* 'Goldflame'	A hybrid perennial vine with purplish stems bearing pairs of oval, 2-in. leaves that are blue-green above and gray-green below. Red flower buds produce 2-lipped, 2-in.-long flowers that are purple-pink on the outside and yellow inside.	●●	Summer	Vine Height: 5–15' Spread: 1–2' Ground cover Height: 1–2' Spacing: 1–2'	4 to 9	Full sun to partial shade. Moist, well-drained soil. Once established, this honeysuckle hybrid tolerates dry soil. Grow it as a sprawling ground cover, or train it on trellises and fences. Prune after flowering if growth becomes too rampant.

			Flower Color	Time of Bloom	Growth Habit	Hardiness Zones	Growing Conditions
	LONICERA TRUMPET HONEYSUCKLE *Lonicera sempervirens*	A woody vine native to the Southeast that is evergreen in warm regions but deciduous in the North. It bears attractive, red-orange, tubular, 2-in. flowers with yellow throats. Cultivars with scarlet or yellow flowers are available.	○ ● ●	Summer	Vine Height: 3–15' Spread: 1–2' Ground cover Height: 1–2' Spacing: 1–2'	4 to 10	Full sun to partial shade. Moist soil. Once established, this honeysuckle species can tolerate dry soil. Grow it as a sprawling ground cover, or train it on trellises and fences. Prune if growth becomes too rampant.
	LUFFA DISHCLOTH GOURD, VEGETABLE-SPONGE *Luffa acutangula*	An annual vine grown for the fibrous inside of its 1-ft.-long, club-shaped gourd fruit, which is used as a sponge when dried. Young fruits are edible. Vines have angular leaves and bear large, 5-petaled, yellow or white flowers.	○ ○	Summer	Vine Height: 8–15' Spread: 5–15' Ground cover Height: 1–2' Spacing: 2–4'	Tender annual	Full sun. Well-drained, sandy loam of average to low fertility. Sow seeds $1/2$ in. deep in late spring after danger of frost has passed. Provide support for vines, or let them sprawl on the ground.
	LYSIMACHIA CREEPING JENNIE, MONEYWORT *Lysimachia nummularia*	A creeping perennial with trailing, rooted stems that bear pairs of penny-size, round, smooth, pale yellow leaves that turn darker green in the shade. Single, $1/2$-in., bright yellow, cup-shaped flowers have 5 petals.	○	Late spring to midsummer	Height: 1–2" Spread: 1–3' Spacing: 1–1$1/2$'	4 to 8	Full sun to partial shade. Moist, humus-rich soil. Lysimachia is easy to grow and adapts to a variety of moist to wet soils. Plants spread rapidly and can become invasive over time. In humid regions they can become weedy.
	MAHONIA CREEPING MAHONIA *Mahonia repens*	A low, spreading evergreen shrub with leaves that have 2–3 pairs of hollylike, spine-tipped leaflets that are dull green in summer and purple in winter. The showy clusters of small, rich yellow flowers at the tips of twigs produce dark blue berries.	○	Spring or autumn, depending on location	Height: 1–3' Spread: 1–5' Spacing: 1–2'	5 to 8	Full sun to partial shade; grows best in partial sun. Moist, humus-rich, acid, well-drained soil. In cold regions, protect plants from drying winter winds.
	MANDEVILLA MANDEVILLA ◄ *Mandevilla × amabilis* CHILEAN JASMINE *M. laxa*	Tropical, woody, twining vines with fragrant, 5-lobed, trumpet-shaped, showy flowers and glossy, heart-shaped or oblong leaves. Evergreen M. × amabilis has deep rose-colored flowers. Deciduous M. laxa has white or cream-colored flowers.	○ ●	M. × amab. Spring to autumn M. laxa Summer	Height: 10–20' Spread: 5–10' Spacing: 2–4'	M. × amab. 10 to 11 M. laxa 8 to 11	Full sun. Moist, humus-rich soil. Provide support for vines. Mandevilla can be grown in tubs.

◄ Indicates species shown

Ground Covers & Vines

			Flower Color	Time of Bloom	Growth Habit	Hardiness Zones	Growing Conditions
	MENTHA CORSICAN MINT, CREME-DE-MENTHE PLANT *Mentha requienii*	A low-growing perennial ground cover whose ¼- to ½-in., bright green, rounded leaves have a very strong mint flavor. The smooth stems creep along the ground and bear tubular, 2-lipped, lavender flowers.	●	Summer	Height: 1–4" Spread: 1–2' Spacing: 6–12"	6 to 11	Full sun to partial shade. Humus-rich, moist soil. Corsican mint, unlike other mints, is not invasive; it spreads slowly with age.
	MITCHELLA PARTRIDGEBERRY *Mitchella repens*	An eastern native ground cover effective in cool, shady sites. Pairs of round, dark green leaves with white veins line the sprawling stems. Trumpet-shaped white flowers produce red fruits.	○	Late spring to early summer	Height: 1–2" Spread: 1–2' Spacing: 6–12"	4 to 9	Partial sun to full shade. Cool, moist, humus-rich, acid soil; sites among pines and hemlocks are ideal. Partridge-berry can be grown indoors in containers year-round.
	MYOSOTIS FORGET-ME-NOT *Myosotis scorpioides*	An early-spring-blooming perennial that produces clusters of clear blue, 5-petaled flowers with yellow or white centers. The light green leaves and stems form a matlike cover.	●	Early spring to midsummer	Height: 3–6" Spread: 1–2' Spacing: 1–1½'	3 to 9	Dappled sun to partial shade, with some afternoon shade in warm climates. Well-drained, evenly moist soil. Myosotis does not tolerate drought well. Plants spread rapidly in moist, shady sites and grow well alongside shallow water.
	OMPHALODES CREEPING FORGET-ME-NOT, NAVELWORT *Omphalodes verna*	A creeping perennial ground cover that is evergreen in warm climates. It forms clumps of lance-shaped or oval leaves and bears loose clusters of ½-in., 5-lobed, sky blue, forget-me-not-like flowers. White-flowered cultivars are available.	○ ●	Spring	Height: 6–8" Spread: 1–2' Spacing: 1–1½'	5 to 8	Full sun to partial shade. Moist, humus-rich, slightly acid, well-drained soil.
	OPHIOPOGON WHITE LILYTURF ◀ *Ophiopogon jaburan* DWARF LILYTURF *O. japonicus*	Grasslike, evergreen perennials whose leaves form sprawling mounds. O. jaburan has clusters of 6-petaled white flowers and 1½- to 2-ft.-long leaves; O. japonicus has lilac flowers and 1- to 1½-ft.-long leaves.	○ ●	Mid- to late summer	Height: 8–12" Spread: 1–2' Spacing: 1–1½'	7 to 11	Partial sun to full shade; both species grow well in shady, moist sites in zones 9–11 but can take more sun in colder regions. Moist, well-drained soil. Ophiopogon can be grown as a semiaquatic plant.

			Flower Color	Time of Bloom	Growth Habit	Hardiness Zones	Growing Conditions
	OSTEOSPER-MUM TRAILING AFRICAN DAISY *Osteospermum fruticosum*	*A shrubby perennial with hairy leaves that clasp trailing stems up to 2 ft. long. Daisylike, 1½- to 2-in. flowers have purple centers and white ray petals with violet undersides.*	○	*Intermittent*	Height: 6–12" Spread: 2–4' Spacing: 1–2'	9 to 11 (Grow as an annual in colder regions)	*Full sun. Sandy, well-drained soil. Osteospermum makes an excellent ground cover for dry soil and coastal sites and can also be grown in hanging baskets. Plants spread fairly rapidly.*
	PACHYSANDRA ALLEGHANY SPURGE *Pachysandra procumbens* JAPANESE SPURGE ◄ *P. terminalis*	*Slow-growing evergreen ground covers with whorls of dark, lustrous, large-toothed leaves and short spikes of creamy white flowers. P. terminalis has light green leaves. P. pro-cumbens, deciduous in cold climates, has darker leaves.*	○	*Early spring to early summer*	Height: 6–12" Spread: 1–2' Spacing: 1–2'	3 to 9	*Full sun to deep shade, with some afternoon shade in warm climates; in all climates, partial shade produces the best growth. Well-drained, moist, fertile soil with ample organic matter.*
	PARTHENO-CISSUS VIRGINIA CREEPER *Parthenocissus quinquefolia*	*A woody vine that climbs by tendrils with pads. The deciduous leaves are divided into 5 fingerlike, toothed, 6-in.-long leaflets and turn brilliant red in autumn. Clusters of tiny greenish flowers produce ¼-in. dark blue berries.*	●	*Summer*	Vine Height: 10–50' Spread: 2–3' Ground cover Height: 6–12" Spacing: 1–2'	3 to 9	*Full sun to full shade. Moist, well-drained, humus-rich soil. Virginia creeper will trail along the ground or grow up trees, walls, or trellises. It is easy to grow and untroubled by pests.*
	PARTHENO-CISSUS BOSTON IVY *Parthenocissus tricuspidata*	*A woody vine with decid-uous, 3-lobed leaves that turn brilliant red in autumn. Clusters of tiny greenish flowers produce ¼-in. dark blue berries.*	●	*Summer*	Height: 10–50' Spread: 20–30' Spacing: 4–8'	4 to 8	*Full sun to partial shade, with afternoon shade in hot cli-mates. Not at all choosy about soil conditions. Boston ivy grows vigorously and may need to be pruned from win-dows. Over time, roots may erode masonry joints.*
	PASSIFLORA BLUE PASSION-FLOWER *Passiflora caerulea*	*Perennial vines that climb by tendrils. Leaves have 5–9 lobes. The ornate flowers are pink or white with blue and violet ringlike markings and produce egg-shaped yellow fruits that are 2½ in. long.*	○ ● ●	*Summer to autumn*	Height: 3–15' Spread: 2–6' Spacing: 1–2'	8 to 10	*Full sun. Evenly moist, well-drained soil. Blue passion-flower grows rapidly where sun, moisture, and warmth are abundant. Plants die back to roots at first frost.*

◄ *Indicates species shown*

Ground Covers & Vines

		Flower Color	Time of Bloom	Growth Habit	Hardiness Zones	Growing Conditions
PASSIFLORA MAYPOP, WILD PASSION- FLOWER *Passiflora incarnata*	A native perennial vine of the Southeast with leaves that have 3 fingerlike lobes. The 2- to 3-in.-wide, ornate flowers have 5 white petals streaked with lavender and purple; they produce 2-in.-long, egg-shaped, edible yellow fruits.	○ ◔	Summer	Height: 3–15' Spread: 2–6' Spacing: 1–2'	7 to 9	Full sun. Evenly moist, well-drained soil. Wild passionflower grows rapidly where sun, moisture, and warmth are abundant. Mulch plants during winter in zone 7.
PHALARIS RIBBON GRASS *Phalaris arundinacea* var. *picta*	A fast-growing perennial grass whose spreading shoots and towering 7-in. spikes of soft white or pink flowers add drama to garden borders. The broad (³/₄- to 1-in.-wide), flat leaves have creamy white edges.	○ ◔	Late spring to early summer	Height: 2–5' Spread: 6–12" Spacing: 6–12"	4 to 9	Partial sun to partial shade, with afternoon shade in warm climates. Moist, even waterlogged soil; plants will grow under several inches of standing water.
PHASEOLUS SCARLET RUNNER BEAN *Phaseolus coccineus*	A climbing, twining vine that bears brilliant scarlet, showy, 1-in., pealike flowers and leaves with 3 leaflets. The edible pods and seeds are a bonus.	●	Summer	Height: 8–15' Spread: 6–8" Spacing: 4–6"	10 to 11 (Grow as a half-hardy annual in colder regions)	Full sun. Moist, humus-rich, well-drained soil. Grow scarlet runner bean as an annual by planting seeds 1 to 2 in. deep in mid-spring a few weeks before the last frost. Space rows 3 to 4 ft. apart. Provide support for vines.
PHLOX BLUE PHLOX, WILD SWEET WILLIAM ◄ *Phlox divaricata* CREEPING PHLOX *P. stolonifera*	Creeping perennials with lavender-blue flowers and oval leaves. P. divaricata bears loose clusters of 1¹/₂-in. flowers with notched petals on upright stems; the mat-forming P. stolonifera has 1-in. flowers with smooth-edged petals.	◔ ◔	Early spring to early summer	P. divar. Height: 8–18" Spread: 8–12" P. stolon. Height: 4–6" Spread: 1–2'	4 to 8	Filtered sun to full shade. Well-drained, evenly moist, humus-rich, slightly acid soil. These are excellent plants for shady rock gardens or for naturalizing in woodland settings. Space P. divaricata 6 to 12 in. apart; space P. stolonifera 1 to 2 ft. apart.
PHLOX MOSS PINK *Phlox subulata*	A mound-forming evergreen perennial with needlelike ¹/₂- to 1-in.-long leaves on trailing stems. Showy, pink, white, or lavender, ³/₄-in., tubular flowers each have 5 notched petals.	○ ◔ ◔	Early summer	Height: 3–6" Spread: 6–12" Spacing: 6–12"	4 to 9	Full sun to partial shade. Humus-rich, evenly moist, well-drained soil. Trim foliage in late summer after flowering is over. Moss pink will spread slowly over time.

		Flower Color	Time of Bloom	Growth Habit	Hardiness Zones	Growing Conditions
POLYGONUM CHINA FLEECE VINE, SILVER LACE VINE *Polygonum aubertii*	A fast-growing, twining, woody, deciduous vine with bright green, 1½- to 2½-in., oval, lance-shaped leaves. Lacy, long, slender racemes of tiny, white or pink, fragrant flowers appear near the tips of branches.	⬤	Late summer to early autumn	Height: 10–25' Spread: 5–15' Spacing: 4–8'	5 to 9	Full sun. Well-drained, evenly moist soil. Polygonum is a vigorously growing plant that spreads rapidly from underground stems; it can become weedy under ideal conditions. Prune in early spring.
PULMONARIA COWSLIP LUNGWORT *Pulmonaria angustifolia* COMMON LUNGWORT ◀ *P. officinalis*	Attractive perennial ground covers with mottled, hairy leaves and 5-petaled flowers held above the foliage. P. angustifolia *has blue flowers and narrow leaves.* Wide-leaved P. officinalis *has violet, blue, white, or red flowers.*	⬤	Spring	Height: 8–18" Spread: 2–3' Spacing: 1–2'	4 to 8	Partial to full shade. Moist, humus-rich soil that never completely dries out. Pulmonaria may be troubled by slugs and snails. Divide periodically to stimulate vigorous growth and flowering.
PULMONARIA BETHLEHEM SAGE *Pulmonaria saccharata*	A perennial ground cover bearing hairy, semievergreen leaves with white spots. Clusters of light blue, white, or red flowers turn pink as they age. 'Mrs. Moon' is a very hardy, low-growing cultivar.	⬤	Early spring	Height: 1–1½' Spread: 2–3' Spacing: 1–2'	3 to 8	Full shade. Moist, humus-rich soil that never completely dries out. Pulmonaria may be troubled by slugs and snails. Divide periodically to stimulate vigorous growth and flowering.
PYRACANTHA SCARLET FIRE THORN *Pyracantha coccinea*	An evergreen shrub with narrow, dark green, 1- to 2-in. leaves. Stems bear ½-in. thorns. Clusters of small white flowers in spring produce brilliant red, orange-red, or yellow berries in fall.	○	Spring	Height: 6–18' Spread: 6–18' Spacing: 2–4'	6 to 9	Full sun. Well-drained soil; tolerates dry soil in summer. Disease and insects can be problems. Pyracantha is spectacular espaliered against a wall.
ROSA CLIMBING ROSE *Rosa hybrids*	Climbers with long canes (erect, thin stems) that bear small groups of large (3- to 3½-in.), fragrant flowers. Many cultivars are available. 'City of York' has white flowers; 'New Dawn' has light pink flowers.	⬤	Summer	Height: 10–30' Spread: 5–20' Spacing: 3–6'	4 to 10	Full sun to very light shade. Fertile, evenly moist, well-drained, humus-rich soil with near-neutral pH (6–7). Prune lightly after flowering ends, removing ⅔ of side-shoot growth. Do not cut the central stem. Train these roses on walls or fences.

◀ *Indicates species shown*

Ground Covers & Vines

		Flower Color	Time of Bloom	Growth Habit	Hardiness Zones	Growing Conditions
ROSA RAMBLER ROSE *Rosa* hybrids	A hybrid rose with long, flexible canes that bear large clusters of small (1- to 1½-in.) flowers. 'American Pillar' has pink, scentless flowers; pink-flowered 'Paul's Himalayan Musk' is slightly fragrant.	○	Late summer	Height: 10–20' Spread: 2–4' Spacing: 1–3'	4 to 10	Full sun to very light shade. Fertile, evenly moist, well-drained, humus-rich soil with near-neutral pH (6–7). Prune lightly after flowering ends, removing withered flower clusters. Rambler roses are ideal for training on trellises and arches.
ROSA LADY BANKS ROSE *Rosa banksiae*	A nearly thornless, climbing, evergreen rose with 2-in., glossy green leaves divided into 3–5 pointed leaflets. The 1- to 2-in.-wide, yellow or white flowers produce ¼-in. red fruits (hips). Single- or double-flowered cultivars are available.	○	Spring to early summer	Height: 10–20' Spread: 2–4' Spacing: 2–3'	7 to 8	Full sun to very light shade. Fertile, evenly moist, well-drained, humus-rich soil with near-neutral pH (6–7). Lady Banks rose is ideal for training on arbors and fences.
ROSA MEMORIAL ROSE *Rosa wichuraiana*	A sprawling, trailing, semi-evergreen, thorny rose with glossy leaves that have 5–11 small, round leaflets. Fragrant, white, 1½- to 2-in.-wide flowers are borne in small clusters.	○	Late spring to late autumn	Height: 10–20' Spread: 2–4' Spacing: 2–3'	6 to 8	Full sun to very light shade. Fertile, evenly moist, well-drained, humus-rich soil with near-neutral pH (6–7). Memorial rose is ideal for training on arbors and fences or for use as a ground cover.
ROSMARINUS CREEPING ROSEMARY *Rosmarinus officinalis* 'Prostratus'	A tender, evergreen perennial shrub with scaly gray bark and pairs of needlelike, ¾-in. leaves that are dark green above and pale below. It is used as a culinary or cosmetic herb. Low-growing 'Prostratus' is an aromatic ground cover.	●	Early summer	Height: 1–2' Spread: 3–6' Spacing: 2–4'	8 to 11 (Grow as a half-hardy annual in zone 7 and colder)	Full sun to partial shade. Deep, sandy, well-drained soil. Propagate plants from cuttings. Scale insects and mealybugs can be problems. *Rosmarinus* can be grown as an indoor container plant over winter, but use a big pot for its extensive roots.
RUBUS BRAMBLE, FLOWERING BLACK-BERRY *Rubus calycinoides* (*R. pentalobus*)	A trailing, creeping evergreen perennial with puckered, 1½-in.-wide, rounded, geranium-like leaves. The small (¼- to ½-in.) white flowers produce salmon-colored to purple fruits, depending on the cultivar.	○	Mid- to late summer	Height: 2–4" Spread: 2–6' Spacing: 1½–3'	7 to 9	Full sun to partial shade. Sandy, well-drained soil of average fertility. Flowering blackberry is drought tolerant once established. Plants spread by rooting from tips of canes (long stems).

			Flower Color	Time of Bloom	Growth Habit	Hardiness Zones	Growing Conditions
SANTOLINA LAVENDER COTTON ◀ *Santolina chamae-cyparissus* GREEN SANTOLINA *S. virens*		*Perennial shrubs whose divided, 1¼-in., evergreen leaves have a musky lavender scent. Tiny yellow flowers are clustered into ½-in., buttonlike heads. S. chamaecyparissus has silvery gray leaves; those of S. virens are deep green.*	○	Late spring to early summer	Height: 1½–2' Spread: 6–12" Spacing: 6–12"	8 to 11 (Grow as an annual in zone 7 and colder)	*Full sun to partial shade. Deep, sandy, well-drained soil. Propagate plants from cuttings. Scale insects and mealybugs can be problems. Santolina spp. can be grown indoors in pots over winter, but use big containers for their extensive roots.*
SCHIZO-PHRAGMA JAPANESE HYDRANGEA VINE *Schizophragma hydrangeoides*		*A woody, climbing, decid-uous vine whose 4-in.-wide, heart-shaped, toothed leaves have pale undersides. White, 1½-in. flowers are borne in 8- to 10-in.-wide clusters.*	○	Summer	Height: 10–30' Spread: 2–3' Spacing: 1–2'	5 to 9	*Full sun to partial shade. Evenly moist, well-drained soil of average fertility. Provide support for vines; they tend to produce fewer flowers if grown on the ground.*
SEDUM GOLD MOSS ◀ *Sedum acre* STONECROP *S. spurium* 'Dragon's Blood'		*Mat-forming perennial ground covers with ½-in.-wide flowers and succulent leaves. Evergreen S. acre has bright yellow flowers in small clusters. Semiever-green S. spurium 'Dragon's Blood' has red-tipped leaves and red flowers.*	○ ●	S. acre Late spring to summer S. spur. Late summer	Height: 4–6" Spread: 1–2' Spacing: 1–1½'	3 to 9	*Full sun to partial shade. Well-drained, humus-rich soil. Both types grow well with little care.*
SEMPERVIVUM HEN-AND-CHICKENS, HOUSELEEK *Sempervivum tectorum*		*A succulent, evergreen perennial with light green, flat leaves arranged in 3- to 4-in., cuplike whorls. The pointed leaves often have purple tips. Clusters of purple-red flowers grow on stems that rise 1 ft. above the rosettes of foliage.*	● ●	Early to mid-summer	Height: 3–6" Spread: 4–8" Spacing: 3–6"	5 to 9	*Full sun. Well-drained soil. Plants are quite drought tol-erant; they are prone to rot if soil is overly moist. Semper-vivum needs little care and is an excellent slow-growing ground cover or rock garden plant.*
SOLANUM POTATO VINE *Solanum jasminoides*		*A woody twining vine that is evergreen where winters are mild. The 1- to 3-in.-long, oval leaves are deeply lobed. Bluish white, 1-in.-wide, star-shaped flowers have 5 yellow anthers at their centers and are borne in clusters of 8–12.*	○	Spring; periodically throughout the year	Height: 10–30' Spread: 1–5' Spacing: 1–2'	10 to 11 (Grow as a tender annual in zone 9 and colder)	*Full sun to partial shade. Evenly moist, well-drained, slightly acid soil. Prune back plants to promote vigorous flowering and to keep ram-pant shoots in check.*

◀ *Indicates species shown*

Ground Covers & Vines

		Flower Color	Time of Bloom	Growth Habit	Hardiness Zones	Growing Conditions
SOLEIROLIA BABY'S-TEARS *Soleirolia soleirolii*	A mat-forming, creeping perennial with small (¼-in.), rounded, lush green leaves and inconspicuous flowers. It spreads by rooting from the trailing stems. Use as a ground cover in warm climates or under greenhouse benches.	○	Inconspicuous flowers	Height: 1–4" Spread: 1–2' Spacing: 4–8"	9 to 11	Partial to full shade. Evenly moist, well-drained soil. Baby's-tears is frost sensitive but will regrow quickly in warm weather. Plants may become weedy under ideal growth conditions.
STACHYS LAMB'S-EARS *Stachys byzantina*	A slowly creeping perennial with soft, woolly, silvery leaves and small, purple, 2-lipped flowers. This low ground cover forms dense clumps with age.	●	Late spring to midsummer	Height: 6–18" Spread: 6–12" Spacing: 6–12"	5 to 8	Full sun to partial shade. Well-drained soil. Stachys tends to rot under soggy conditions. Mulch during winter in zone 6 and colder.
TAXUS SPREADING ENGLISH YEW *Taxus baccata* 'Repandens'	A dwarf form of an ever-green, coniferous, multi-stemmed tree with flaky russet bark and ½- to 1-in., flat needles, dark green on top and lime green below. Female trees bear poisonous black seeds surrounded by bright red fleshy cones.		No flowers	Height: 2–6' Spread: 12–15' Spacing: 5–10'	5 to 7	Full sun to full shade. Fertile, evenly moist, well-drained, acid soil. Spreading English yew will not tolerate soggy soil. Protect plants from dry winter winds. Deer browsing may be a problem.
TECOMARIA CAPE HONEYSUCKLE *Tecomaria capensis*	An evergreen, vinelike shrub with 6-in., lush, deep green, compound leaves and strik-ing clusters of orange or scarlet, narrow, tubular, 2-in.-long, 5-lobed flowers borne at the ends of branches. Yellow-flowered cultivars are available.	● ●	Most of year	Vine Height: 4–20' Spread 2–20' Ground cover Height: 1½–2' Spacing: 2–8'	9 to 11	Full sun to partial shade. Evenly moist, well-drained soil. Plants are drought tol-erant once established. Train Cape honeysuckle to grow up fences and trellises, or allow it to sprawl on banks as a ground cover.
THUNBERGIA BLACK-EYED SUSAN VINE *Thunbergia alata*	A fast-growing vine bearing a profusion of golden, 5-lobed, pouched flowers with dark purple centers. The 2-in., toothed, heart-shaped leaves are attractive as well.		Early summer to early autumn	Height: 5–10' Spread: 1–2' Spacing: 6–18"	10 to 11 (Grow as a tender annual in colder regions)	Full sun to partial shade. Moist, well-drained, humus-rich soil. In zone 9 and warmer, sow seeds outdoors in early spring. Elsewhere start indoors 6 to 8 weeks before last frost. Thunbergia grows best on trellises and fences or in hanging baskets.

		Flower Color	Time of Bloom	Growth Habit	Hardiness Zones	Growing Conditions
THYMUS WILD THYME *Thymus serpyllum*	A low, shrubby, herb grown as an aromatic ground cover. Rosy or lilac, tubular, 1/4-in. flowers are gathered in 1/2-in. clusters at tips of hairy stems. The fragrant 1/4-in. leaves can be substituted for those of common thyme in cooking.	●	Late spring to early summer	Height: 1–4" Spread: 1–2' Spacing: 6–12"	5 to 9	Full sun to partial shade. Well-drained soil of average fertility. Wild thyme spreads slowly, filling space between stones in walks and rock gardens.
TIARELLA FOAMFLOWER *Tiarella cordifolia*	An evergreen perennial ground cover forming mounds of fuzzy, heart-shaped, light green leaves with sharp lobes that turn coppery bronze in autumn and winter. Foamy spikes of 5-petaled white flowers are held above the foliage.	○	Late spring	Height: 8–12" Spread: 9–15" Spacing: 9–15"	3 to 8	Full shade. Moist, humus-rich soil; sites under deciduous trees are ideal. Tiarella will not tolerate dry soil, but adapts to normal garden conditions if shade is provided. Plants spread slowly with age. Slugs can be a problem.
TRACHE-LOSPERMUM CONFEDERATE JASMINE, STAR JASMINE *Trachelospermum jasminoides*	A slow-growing, twining, evergreen vine with pairs of 2- to 3-in.-long, oval, pointed, leathery, lustrous leaves. Fragrant, 5-petaled, 1-in. white flowers are borne in loose clusters.	○	Mid- to late spring	Height: 10–30' Spread: 3–5' Spacing: 1–2'	8 to 9	Partial sun. Evenly moist, humus-rich, well-drained soil. Provide support for vines, or allow star jasmine to sprawl over the ground for use as a ground cover. Prune old plants periodically to reduce old wood.
TROPAEOLUM NASTURTIUM *Tropaeolum majus*	A tender annual with showy, edible flowers and foliage. The yellow or orange, 2- to 3-in. flowers are often spotted or streaked with red. Both trailing vine and dwarf bush forms are available.		Summer to frost	Height: 1–10' Spread: 1–10' Spacing: 1–3'	Tender annual	Full sun to partial shade. Average, well-drained soil. For the most abundant flowering, do not add fertilizer. Nasturtiums grow best in cool weather. Sow seeds directly where plants are desired after all danger of frost has passed.
TROPAEOLUM CANARY-BIRD FLOWER, CANARY CREEPER *Tropaeolum peregrinum*	A fast-growing, sprawling vine bearing pale yellow, fringed, irregular, 1-in.-wide flowers with long, green-spurred lower petals. The 4-in., deeply cleft leaves resemble bird's feet.		Summer to frost	Height: 5–8' Spread: 1–1½' Spacing: 6–18"	Tender annual	Full sun to partial shade. Evenly moist, well-drained soil of average fertility. This vine grows best in cool weather. Sow seeds directly where plants are desired after danger of frost is past. Provide support for vines, or use as a ground cover.

◀ *Indicates species shown*

Ground Covers & Vines

			Flower Color	Time of Bloom	Growth Habit	Hardiness Zones	Growing Conditions
	VERONICA CREEPING SPEEDWELL *Veronica repens*	A mosslike, mat-forming perennial with ¼- to ½-in., glossy, light green leaves and small clusters of delicate, pale blue, ¼-in. flowers. White- or pink-flowered cultivars are available.	○ ●	Spring	Height: 2–4" Spread: 1–3' Spacing: 6–12"	4 to 8	Full sun to partial shade. Moist soil of average fertility. V. repens spreads rapidly and may become weedy in lawns. Plants can withstand some foot traffic.
	VINCA PERIWINKLE *Vinca major* 'Variegata' ◄ *V. minor*	Evergreen ground covers with thin, sprawling stems and pairs of glossy, leathery, dark green or variegated leaves. Lavender-blue, 5-petaled flowers grow singly above mats of foliage and are 2 in. wide in V. major and ¾ in. wide in V. minor.	● ●	Mid-spring to early summer	Height: 4–6" Spread: 10–24" Spacing: 8–16"	4 to 8	Full sun to full shade, with some afternoon shade in warm climates. Any type of soil except dry. V. major 'Variegata' is often grown as an annual in containers.
	VIOLA SWEET VIOLET *Viola odorata*	A perennial with fragrant, ½-in.-wide, purple or white flowers that rise on stalks above 2-in., downy leaves. The lowest of the 5 petals has a spur laden with nectar and sweet perfume.	○ ● ●	Spring	Height: 4–12" Spread: 6–12" Spacing: 6–12"	5 to 9	Full to partial shade. Moist, humus-rich soil. Sweet violet creeps slowly by rhizome growth or self-seeding. Under ideal conditions plants may become rampant. Mildew and slugs may be problems.
	VITIS GRAPE ◄ *Vitis* spp. CRIMSON GLORY VINE *V. coignetiae*	Rapidly growing, deciduous, woody vines that climb by tendrils. The attractive, shreddy bark is red-brown. Small clusters of tiny green flowers produce clusters of grapes. V. coignetiae has 1-ft. leaves that turn bright red in autumn.	●	Summer	Height: 10–50' Spread: 5–15' Spacing: 3–6'	V. spp. 3 to 10 V. coig. 6 to 9	Full sun to partial shade. Evenly moist, humus-rich, well-drained, fertile soil. Provide support for vines. Prune back in late winter to encourage vigorous growth.
	WISTERIA JAPANESE WISTERIA ◄ *Wisteria floribunda* CHINESE WISTERIA *W. sinensis*	Vigorously growing woody vines bearing compound leaves 10 to 15 in. long with 13–19 leaflets. Fragrant, 1- to 2-in., pealike flowers are borne in clusters 1 ft. or longer. W. floribunda has violet flowers; those of W. sinensis are bluish.	● ●	Mid-spring	Height: 20–50' Spread: 4–8' Spacing: 3–6'	W. flor. 4 to 9 W. sin. 5 to 8	Full sun. Moist, well-drained, humus-rich soil. Do not apply nitrogen fertilizer; wisteria grows better without it. Vines can grow rampantly; heavy pruning may be needed to keep them under control.

Plant Hardiness Zone Map

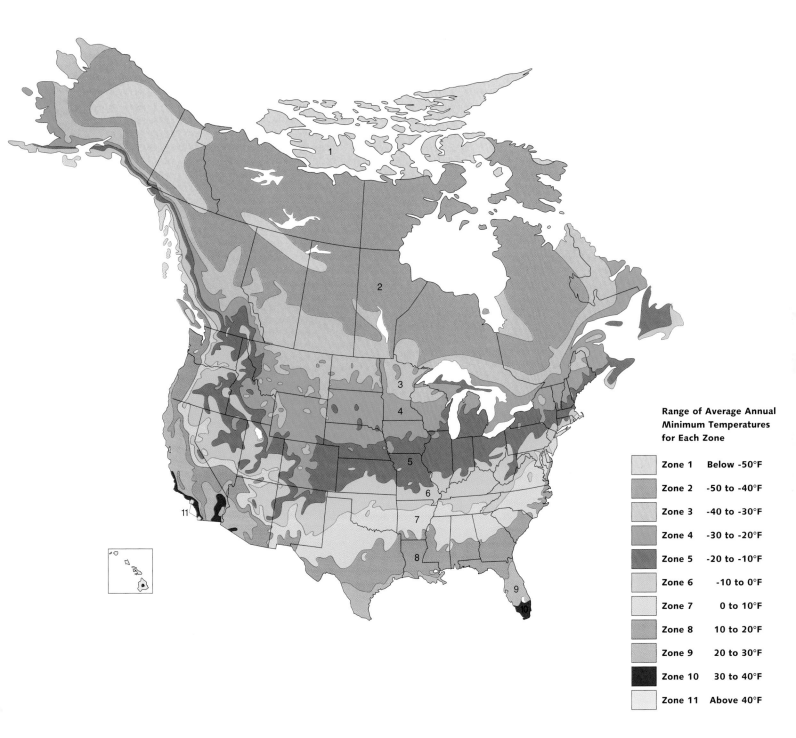

Range of Average Annual Minimum Temperatures for Each Zone

	Zone 1	Below -50°F
	Zone 2	-50 to -40°F
	Zone 3	-40 to -30°F
	Zone 4	-30 to -20°F
	Zone 5	-20 to -10°F
	Zone 6	-10 to 0°F
	Zone 7	0 to 10°F
	Zone 8	10 to 20°F
	Zone 9	20 to 30°F
	Zone 10	30 to 40°F
	Zone 11	Above 40°F

Resources for Lawns, Ground Covers & Vines

There are many dependable mail-order suppliers that can be helpful for gardeners interested in lawns, ground covers, and vines. A selection is included here. Most have catalogues available upon request (some charge a fee). An excellent source of further resources is Gardening by Mail *by Barbara J. Barton. Updates on each edition are provided three times a year, available through subscription (forms provided in back of book); a new edition comes out every few years. To obtain this book, check your local bookstore or contact the publisher: Houghton Mifflin Co., 222 Berkeley Street, Boston, MA 02116. Telephone: (617) 351-5000.*

Seeds & Plants

Kurt Bluemel, Inc.
2740 Greene Lane
Baldwin, MD 21013
310-557-7229
Extensive collection of perennials and grasses.

Bluestone Perennials
7211 Middle Ridge Road
Madison, OH 44057
800-852-5243
Perennials and selected shrubs and ground covers.

DeGiorgi Seed Company
6011 N Street
Omaha, NE 68117-1634
800-858-2580
Broad selection of seeds as well as books and garden supplies.

Henry Field's Seed & Nursery
415 N. Burnett Street
Shenandoah, IA 51602
605-665-9391
Seeds, supplies, and plants.

Forest Farm
990 Tetherow Road
Williams, OR 97544
503-846-6963
Huge selection of plants, including ground covers and vines.

Garden Solutions
617 Garden Terrace
Holland, MI 49422-9030
616-771-9540
Live plants, including vines and ground covers.

Greenlee Nursery
301 E. Franklin Avenue
Pomona, CA 91766
909-629-9045
Sedges, rushes, grasses, and ground covers.

Gurney's Seed & Nursery Co.
110 Capital Street
Yankton, SD 57079
605-665-4451
Seeds, plants, and tools.

Holbrook Farm & Nursery
115 Lance Road
P.O. Box 368
Fletcher, NC 28732
704-891-7790
Catalogue of perennials, including many ground covers.

Jackson & Perkins
P.O. Box 1028
Medford, OR 97501
800-292-4769
Many perennials, including ground covers.

J. W. Jung Seed Co.
335 S. High Street
Randolph, WI 53957
414-326-4100
Extensive catalogue that includes ground covers and dwarf shrubs.

Lake County Nursery
Box 122
Perry, OH 44081
216-259-5571
Extensive catalogue, including ground covers and vines.

Mellinger's Inc.
2310 W. South Range Road
North Lima, OH 44452
800-321-7444
Seeds, plants, books, supplies, and tools.

Milaeger's Gardens
4838 Douglas Avenue
Racine, WI 53402
800-669-9956
Many perennials, including a selection of vines.

Musser Forests Inc.
P.O. Box 340
Indiana, PA 15701
412-465-5686
Live plants, including ground covers and some vines.

Native Gardens
5737 Fisher Lane
Greenback, TN 37742
615-856-0220
Nursery-propagated native perennials, including vines and ground covers.

Powell's Gardens
Route 3, Box 21
Princeton, NC 27569
919-936-4421
Broad selection of perennials and ornamental trees, shrubs, and vines.

Seeds Trust
High Altitude Gardens
P.O. Box 4619
Ketchum, ID 83340
800-874-7333
Organically grown seeds, including grasses.

Spring Hill
110 West Elm Street
Tipp City, OH 45371
800-582-8527
Extensive collection of perennials, including many ground covers.

Springvale Farm Nursery
Mozier Hollow Road
Hamburg, IL 62045
618-232-1108
Ground covers, perennials, tools, and supplies.

Thompson & Morgan
P.O. Box 1308
Jackson, NJ 08527-0308
800-274-7333
Extensive seed collection
for all plant types.

Van Bourgondien & Sons
245 Farmingdale Road
Babylon, NY 11702
800-552-9996
Bulbs and perennials,
including many ground
covers.

André Viette
Route 1, Box 16
Fishersville, VA 22939
703-943-2315
Perennials, including some
ground covers and climb-
ing plants.

Wayside Gardens
P.O. Box 1
Hodges, SC 29695
800-845-1124
Ornamental perennials,
trees, shrubs, and ground
covers.

White Flower Farm
P.O. Box 50
Litchfield, CT 06759
203-496-9600
Catalogue featuring an
extensive collection of
perennials.

Supplies & Accessories

Alsto's Handy Helpers
P.O. Box 1267
Galesburg, IL 61401
800-447-0048
Practical outdoor products
for yard and garden.

Brookstone
5 Vose Farm Road
Peterborough, NH 03458
800-926-7000
Hard-to-find tools of all
kinds.

Country Home Products
P.O. Box 89
Ferry Road
Charlotte, VT 05445
800-446-8746
Mowers, trimmers, clip-
pers, composters, and var-
ious garden tools.

Garden Way, Inc.
102nd Street & 9th
Avenue
Troy, NY 12180
800-833-6990
Mowers, rotary tillers,
garden carts, and other
types of lawn and garden
equipment.

Gardener's Eden
P.O. Box 7307
San Francisco, CA 94120
800-822-9600
Many items appropriate
for gardeners, including
containers, tools, and
accessories.

Gardener's Supply Co.
128 Intervale Road
Burlington, VT 05401
802-863-1700
Yard and garden supplies
and equipment.

Home Gardener
Manufacturing Company
30 Wright Avenue
Lititz, PA 17543
800-880-2345
Composting and home
gardening equipment.

Langenbach
P.O. Box 1140
El Segundo, CA 90245
800-362-1991
Quality tools for planting
and maintaining yard and
garden.

A. M. Leonard, Inc.
241 Fox Drive
Piqua, OH 45356
800-543-8955
Extensive selection of supplies, tools, and products
for lawns and landscapes.

Walt Nicke's Garden Talk
36 McLeod Lane
P.O. Box 433
Topsfield, MA 01983
800-822-4114
Lawn and garden tools
and supplies.

Smith & Hawken
Two Arbor Lane
Box 6900
Florence, KY 41022-6900
800-776-3336
Well-crafted tools as well
as containers, supplies,
and furniture.

Organic Supplies

Erth-Rite
RD 1, Box 243
Gap, PA 17527
800-332-4171
Fertilizers and various soil
amendments for lawn and
garden.

Gardens Alive!
5100 Schenley Place
Lawrenceburg, IN 47025
812-537-8650
Beneficial insects and a
complete line of supplies
for organic gardening.

Necessary Trading Co.
One Nature's Way
New Castle, VA 24127
703-864-5103
Insecticidal soaps, beneficial insects, botanicals,
traps, and other natural
products.

Peaceful Valley Farm
Supply
P.O. Box 2209
Grass Valley, CA 95945
916-272-4769
Tools and supplies for
organic gardening, includ-
ing lawn seed.

Ringer Corporation
9959 Valley View Road
Eden Prairie, MN 55344
612-941-4180
Organic soil amendments,
beneficial insects, and garden tools.

Safer, Inc.
189 Wells Avenue
Newton, MA 02158
617-964-0842
Pest controls, insecticidal
soaps, and natural and
botanical herbicides.

Seventh Generation
Colchester, VT 05446
800-456-1177
Earth-friendly products for
home and garden.

Index

Photo Credits